At Sylvan, we believe reading is one of life's most important and enriching abilities, and we're glad you've chosen our resources to help your child build these critically important skills. We know that the time you spend with your child reinforcing the lessons learned in school will contribute to his love of reading. This love of reading will translate into academic achievement. A successful reader is ready for the world around him, ready to do research, ready to experience the world of literature, and prepared to make the connections necessary to achieve in school and in life.

We use a research-based, step-by-step process in teaching reading at Sylvan that includes thought-provoking reading selections and activities. As students increase their success as readers they become more confident. With increasing confidence, students build even more success. Our Sylvan workbooks are designed to help you to help your child build the skills and confidence that will contribute to your child's success in school.

Included with your purchase of this workbook is a coupon for a discount at a participating Sylvan center. We hope you will use this coupon to further your child's academic journey. Let us partner with you to support the development of a confident, well prepared, independent learner.

The Sylvan Team

Sylvan Learning Center.
Unleash your child's potential here.

No matter how big or small the academic challenge, every child has the ability to learn. But sometimes children need help making it happen. Sylvan believes every child has the potential to do great things. And, we know better than anyone else how to tap into that academic potential so that a child's future really is full of possibilities. Sylvan Learning Center is the place where your child can build and master the learning skills needed to succeed and unlock the potential you know is there.

The proven, personalized approach of our in-center programs deliver unparalleled results that other supplemental education services simply can't match. Your child's achievements will be seen not only in test scores and report cards but outside the classroom as well. And when he starts achieving his full potential, everyone will know it. You will see a new level of confidence come through in everything he does and every interaction he has.

How can Sylvan's personalized in-center approach help your child unleash his potential?

• Starting with our exclusive Sylvan Skills Assessment®, we pinpoint your child's exact academic needs.

• Then we develop a customized learning plan designed to achieve your child's academic goals.

• Through our method of skill mastery, your child will not only learn and master every skill in his personalized plan, he will be truly motivated and inspired to achieve his full potential.

To get started, included with this Sylvan product purchase is $10 off our exclusive Sylvan Skills Assessment®. Simply use this coupon and contact your local Sylvan Learning Center to set up your appointment.

And to learn more about Sylvan and our innovative in-center programs, call 1-800-EDUCATE or visit www.SylvanLearning.com. *With over 1,000 locations in North America, there is a Sylvan Learning Center near you!*

1st Grade
Super Games & Puzzles

Copyright © 2013 by Sylvan Learning, Inc.

Published in the United States by Random House LLC, New York, and in Canada by Random House of Canada Limited, Toronto.

A Penguin Random House Company

www.tutoring.sylvanlearning.com

The material in this book previously appeared as *First Grade Spelling Games & Activities*, a trade paperback first published by Random House in 2009; *First Grade Vocabulary Puzzles*, a trade paperback first published by Random House in 2009; and *First Grade Math Games & Puzzles*, a trade paperback first published by Random House in 2010.

Source material credits:
Created by Smarterville Productions LLC
Producer: TJ Trochlil McGreevy
Producer & Editorial Direction: The Linguistic Edge
Writers: Margaret Crocker, Sandy Damashek, and Amy Kraft
Cover and Interior Illustrations: Tim Goldman and Duendes del Sur
Layout and Art Direction: SunDried Penguin
Art Manager: Adina Ficano

ISBN: 978-0-8041-2449-2

This book is available at special discounts for bulk purchases for sales promotions or premiums. For more information, write to Special Markets/Premium Sales, 1745 Broadway, MD 6-2, New York, New York 10019, or email specialmarkets@randomhouse.com.

PRINTED IN CHINA

10 9 8 7 6 5 4 3 2 1

Contents

1st Grade
Spelling Games & Activities

Contents

Spell Short A

Slide Words

Let's make words that have a short **a** sound. DRAW a line between each picture and the ending that matches. Then WRITE the first letter of each word.

r am
1

at
2

ap
3

an
4

Around We Go!

CIRCLE the things that have a short **a** sound.

WRITE the words with short **a** on the lines.

_____   _____   _____

Make It Rhyme

CIRCLE the picture that makes a rhyme. WRITE the rhyming word in the space.

The ram eats a _____ .
1

The fan cools the _____ .
2

The hat is on the _____ .
3

Space Walk Words

Make three-letter words with short **a**. START on a blue planet. GO to the green planet. Then GO to another blue planet.

Example:

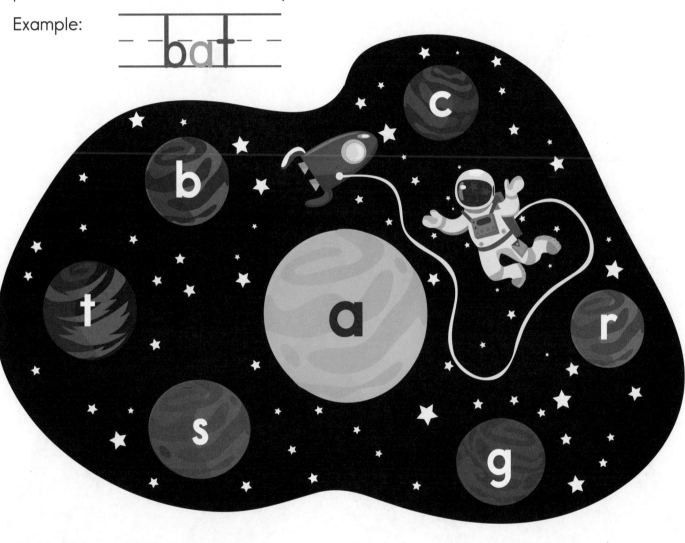

WRITE the words here.

_____ _____ _____

_____ _____ _____

Slide Words

Let's make words that have a short **e** sound. DRAW a line between each picture and the ending that matches. Then WRITE the first letter of each word.

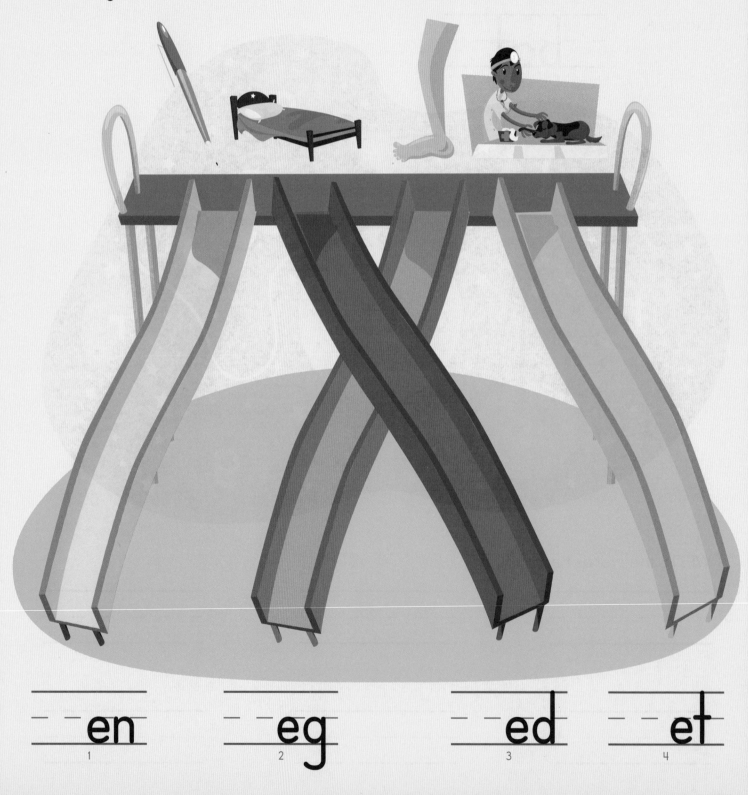

en
1

eg
2

ed
3

et
4

Letter Liftoff

FILL IN the first letter of each short **e** word.

_H_en 1

_b_ed 2

_t_en 3

_P_en 4

_n_et 5

Spell Short E

Around We Go!

CIRCLE the things that have a short **e** sound.

WRITE the words with short **e** on the lines.

_____   _____   _____

_____   _____   _____

Fast Words

Can you SAY this sentence three times fast? Try it!

Ten men fed ten hens.

Now WRITE your own sentence. Use these words or other short **e** words. Then SAY the sentence three times fast!

red   have   beds   legs   red

Make It Rhyme

CIRCLE the picture that makes a rhyme. WRITE the rhyming word in the space.

The wet pet saw the _____.
₁

The hen has a _____.
₂

The bed was _____.
₃

 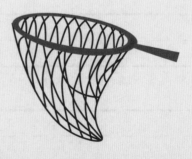

Space Walk Words

Make three-letter words with short **e**. START on a blue planet. GO to the green planet. Then GO to another blue planet.

WRITE the words here.

_____   _____   _____

- - - - - - - - - -   - - - - - - - - - -   - - - - - - - - - -

_____   _____   _____

_____   _____   _____

- - - - - - - - - -   - - - - - - - - - -   - - - - - - - - - -

_____   _____   _____

How Many at the Market?

How many things can we buy at the market? WRITE a number word under each food.

one	two	three	four	five	six	seven	eight

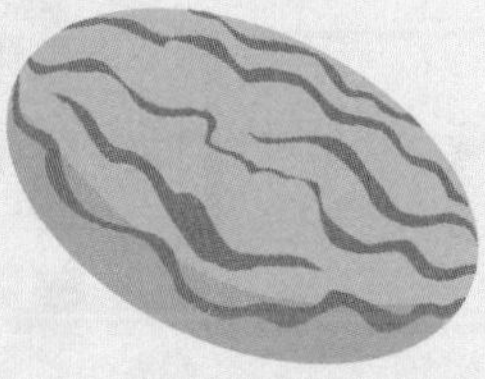

one

1

2

3

4

5

6

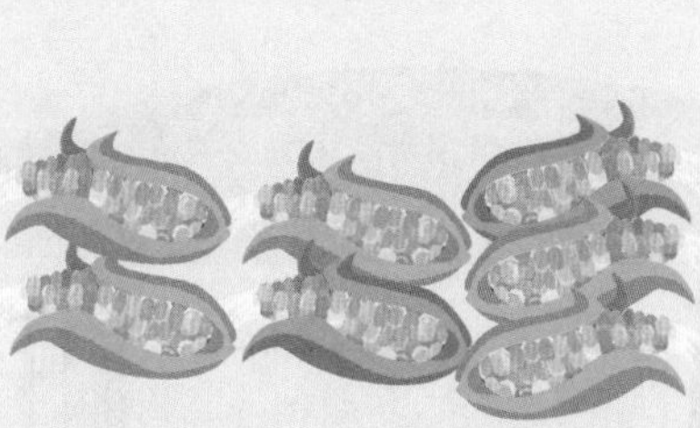

7

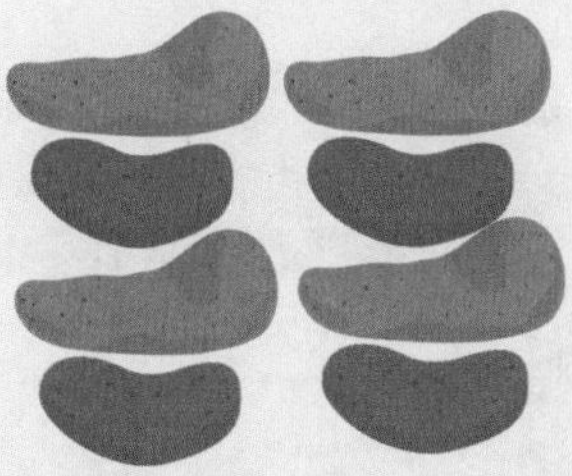

8

Perfect Landing

DRAW a line between each word and its missing vowel. WRITE the vowel in the space.

Soccer Star

DRAW a line between each picture and the matching vowel. WRITE the words in the nets.

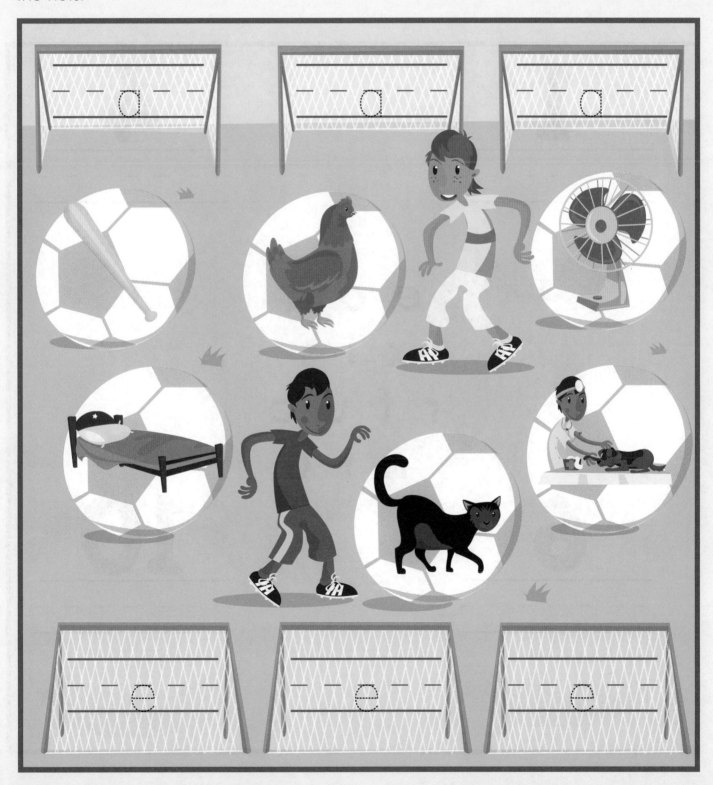

Review

Alphabet Soup

Use the letters in the soup to WRITE the number words. CROSS OUT each letter in the soup after you use it.

1

4

e o n
x i s
r f u o
n t e

6

10

Word Hunt

CIRCLE the **number** words in the grid. WRITE each word after you circle it. Words go across and down.

| one | two | three | four | five | six | seven | eight | nine | ten |

```
n f s e v e n p i h n e
f o n e h i f x m q i k
h u f c d g i b t s n b
y r t e n h v d w i e h
t h r e e t e h o x j t
```

Spell Short I

Slide Words

Let's make words that have a short i sound. DRAW a line between each picture and the ending that matches. Then WRITE the first letter of each word.

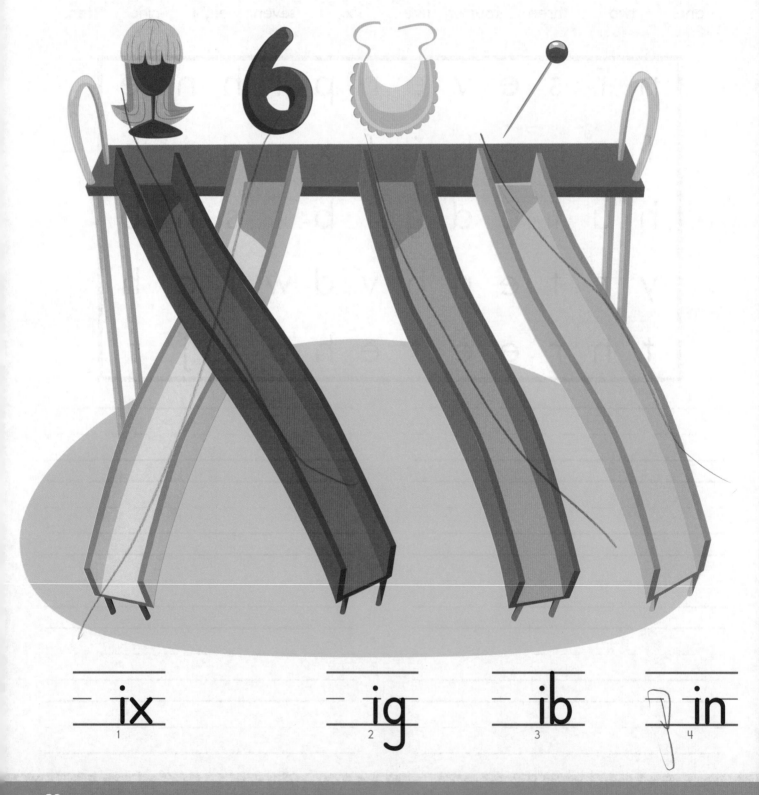

_ _ _ ix
1

_ _ _ ig
2

_ _ _ ib
3

_ _ _ in
4

Around We Go!

CIRCLE the things that have a short **i** sound.

WRITE the words with short **i** on the lines.

_____   _____   _____

- - - - - - - - - -   - - - - - - - - - -   - - - - - - - - - -

_____   _____   _____

Fast Words

Can you SAY this sentence three times fast? Try it!

Six big pigs sit.

Now WRITE your own sentence. Use these words or other short **i** words. Then SAY the sentence three times fast!

| pigs | kids | big | dig |

_____

_____

_____

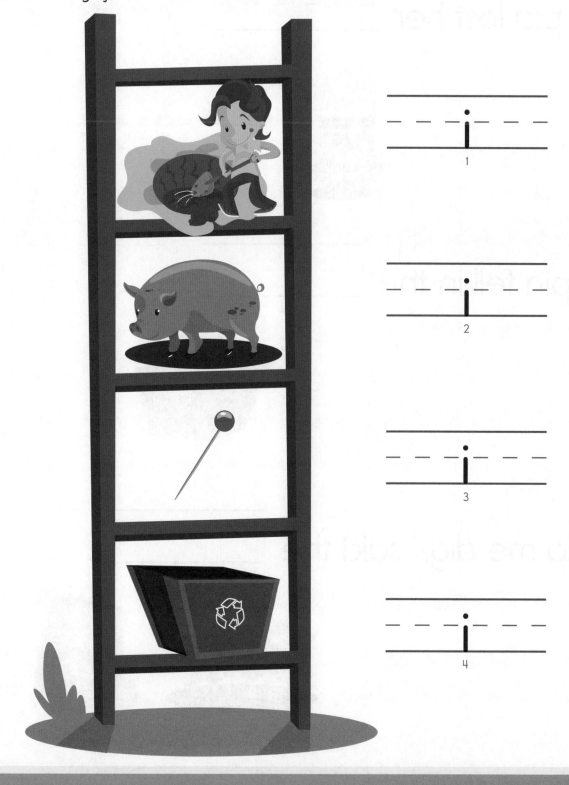

Letter Ladder

Let's make more words with the short **i** sound. IDENTIFY the pictures on the ladder. Then WRITE the words next to the pictures.

HINT: You can change just one letter to make each new word.

i
1

i
2

i
3

i
4

Spell Short I

Make It Rhyme

CIRCLE the picture that makes a rhyme. WRITE the rhyming word in the space.

The pig lost her _____ .
                        1

My pin fell in the _____ .
                          2

"Help me dig," said the _____ .
                                3

Space Walk Words

Make three-letter words with short **i**. START on a blue planet. GO to the orange planet. Then GO to another blue planet.

WRITE the words here.

_____	_____	_____
- - - - - -	- - - - - -	- - - - - -
_____	_____	_____

_____	_____	_____
- - - - - -	- - - - - -	- - - - - -
_____	_____	_____

Slide Words

Let's make words that have a short **o** sound. DRAW a line between each picture and the ending that matches. Then WRITE the first letter of each word.

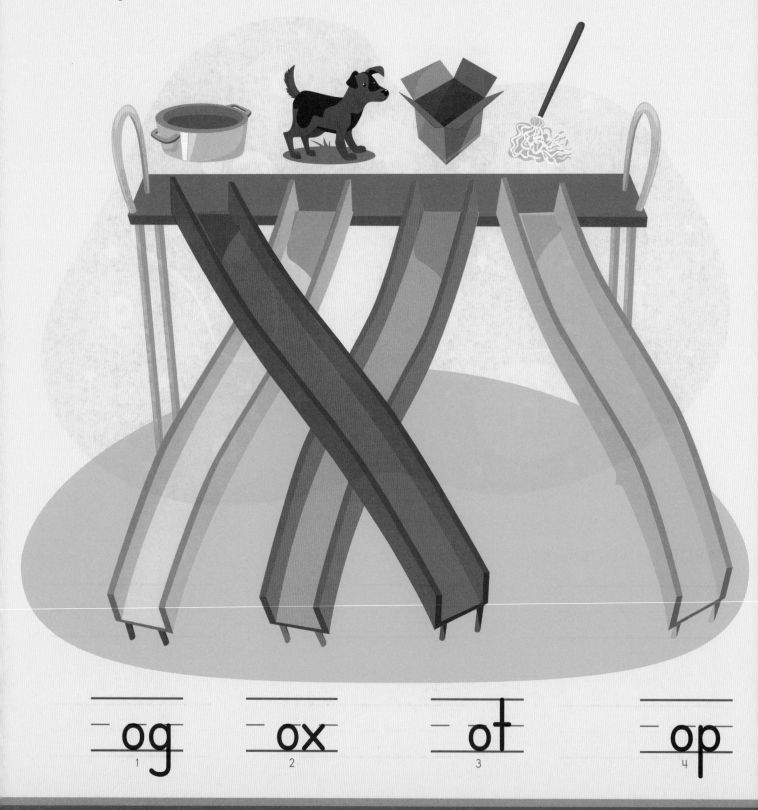

__og
1

__ox
2

__ot
3

__op
4

Letter Ladder

Let's make more words with the short **o** sound. IDENTIFY the pictures on the ladder. Then WRITE the words next to the pictures.

HINT: You can change just one letter to make each new word.

O
1

O
2

O
3

O
4

Make It Rhyme

CIRCLE the picture that makes a rhyme. WRITE the rhyming word in the space.

The dog jumps on a _____ .

The box is on top of the _____ .

Can you hop over the _____ ?

Fast Words

Can you SAY this sentence three times fast? Try it!

Hot pot tops pop.

Now WRITE your own sentence. Use these words or other short **o** words. Then SAY the sentence three times fast!

fox   box   a   mops   the

_____

_ _ _ _ _ _ _ _ _ _ _ _ _ _ _ _ _ _

_____

_ _ _ _ _ _ _ _ _ _ _ _ _ _ _ _ _ _

_____

Spell Short O

Space Walk Words

Make three-letter words with short **o**. START on a blue planet. GO to the green planet. Then GO to another blue planet.

WRITE the words here.

_____ _____ _____

- - - - - - - - - - - - - - - - - - - - - - - - - - - - - - - - -

_____ _____ _____

- - - - - - - - - - - - - - - - - - - - - - - - - - - - - - - - -

Riddle Me This!

UNSCRAMBLE the words to read the riddle.

Q: What ogd pops out of a tpo

_ _ _ _ _   _ _ _ _ _

that is oht?

_ _ _ _ _

A: A hot dog!

Slide Words

Let's make words that have a short **u** sound. DRAW a line between each picture and the ending that matches. Then WRITE the first letter of each word.

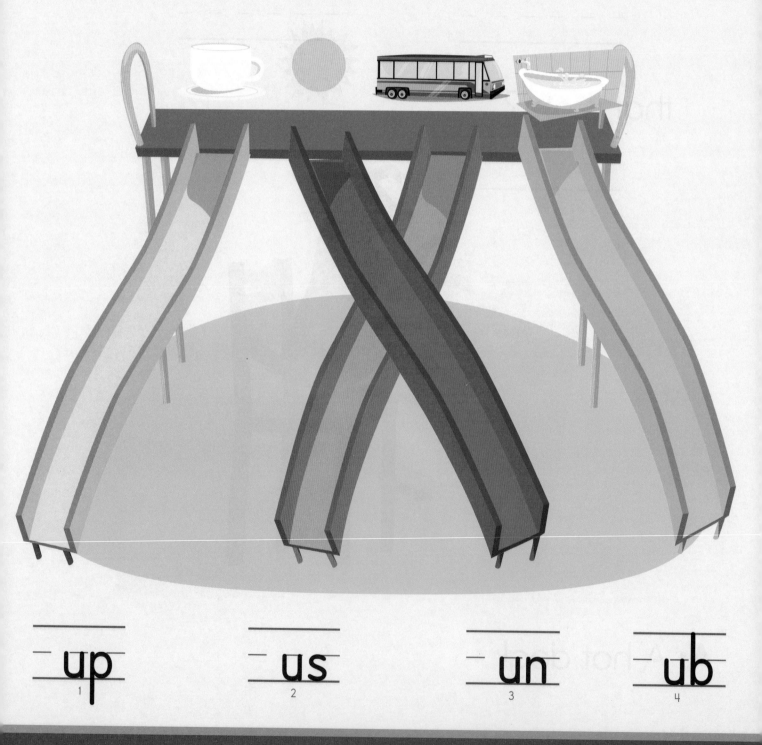

up
1

us
2

un
3

ub
4

Make It Rhyme

CIRCLE the picture that makes a rhyme. WRITE the rhyming word in the space.

The cub jumped in the _____ .

₁

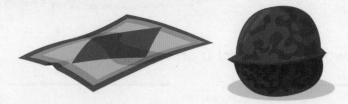

The pup found a _____ .

₂

The bug hid under the _____ .

₃

Around We Go!

CIRCLE the things that have a short **u** sound.

WRITE the words with short **u** on the lines.

_____   _____   _____

Riddle Me This!

UNSCRAMBLE the words in the riddle.

Q: Why did the ubg drive

_____

- - - - -

_____

his usb into the btu?

_____   _____

- - - - -   - - - - -

_____   _____

A: To get wheel-y wet!

Space Walk Words

Make three-letter words with short **u**. START on a blue planet. GO to the green planet. Then GO to another blue planet.

WRITE the words here.

_____   _____   _____

_____   _____   _____

Criss Cross

READ the clues. FILL IN the short **u** words in the boxes.

nut	bug	tub	sun	mud	hut	bus	but	gum

Across

1. A small house is a _____.

3. It takes kids to school.

5. A little insect

7. A _____ has a hard shell.

8. This makes pigs dirty.

Down

2. Where you take a bath

4. The _____ shines in the sky.

5. I ran fast _____ did not win the race.

6. You can chew this.

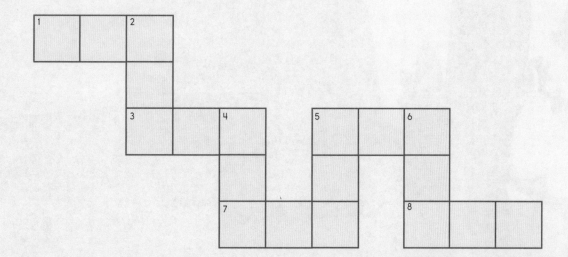

Living Colors

LOOK at all the colors in the market. WRITE a color word under each food.

red   blue   yellow   orange   green   purple   brown   white

_____

- - - - - - - - - - - -

_____
1

_____

- - - - - - - - - - - -

_____
2

_____

- - - - - - - - - - - -

_____
3

_____

- - - - - - - - - - - -

_____
4

_____

- - - - - - - - - - - -

_____
5

_____

- - - - - - - - - - - -

_____
6

_____

- - - - - - - - - - - -

_____
7

_____

- - - - - - - - - - - -

_____
8

Perfect Landing

DRAW a line between each word and the missing vowel. WRITE the vowel in the space.

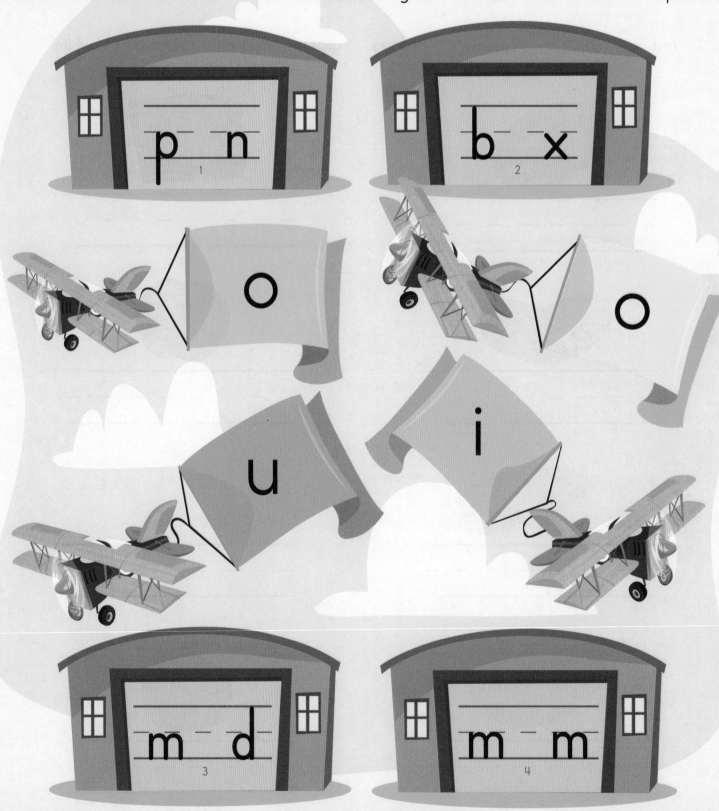

Alphabet Soup

Use the letters in the soup to WRITE the words to match the pictures. CROSS OUT each letter in the soup after you use it.

Fix It!

CHANGE the vowels to fix the signs. WRITE the correct word under each store.

Hets

Bids

1

2

Rogs

Mups

3

4

Bubble Pop

LOOK at the color words in the bubbles. CROSS OUT the words that are misspelled.

yellow

gren

yello

blue

blu

orange

purpel

green

orang

purple

Spell Long A

Slide Words

Let's make words that have a long **a** sound. DRAW a line between each picture and the ending that matches. Then WRITE the first letter of each word.

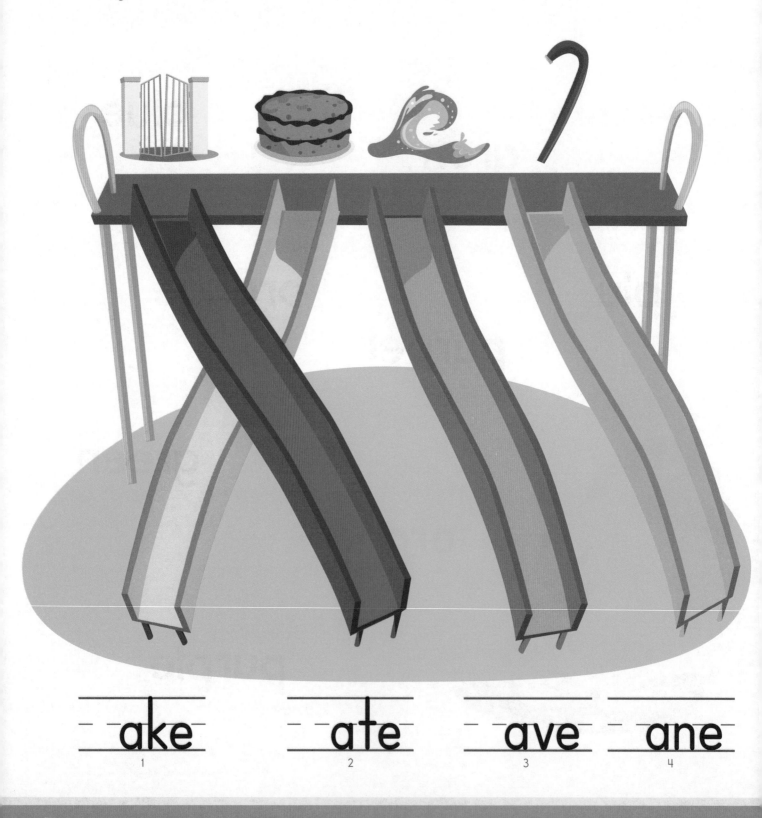

ake
1

ate
2

ave
3

ane
4

Letter Ladder

Let's make more words with the long **a** sound. IDENTIFY the pictures on the ladder. Then WRITE the words next to the pictures.

HINT: You can change just one letter to make each new word.

a   e
1

a   e
2

a   e
3

a   e
4

Around We Go!

CIRCLE the things that have a long **a** sound.

WRITE the words with long **a** on the lines.

_____   _____   _____

_ _ _ _ _ _ _ _   _ _ _ _ _ _ _ _   _ _ _ _ _ _ _ _

_____   _____   _____

Fast Words

Can you SAY this sentence three times fast? Try it!

An ape in a cape came with a cake.

Now WRITE your own sentence. Use these words or other long **a** words. Then SAY the sentence three times fast!

> waves   save   lakes   safe

_____

_ _

_____

_____

Spell Long E and I

Slide Words

Let's make words that have a long **e** or long **i** sound. DRAW a line between each picture and the ending that matches. Then WRITE the first letter of each word.

1. ine
2. ete
3. ite
4. ike

Letter Liftoff

FILL IN the vowel for each long **e** or long **i** word.

P _ te
1

p _ pe
2

b _ ke
3

k _ te
4

n _ ne
5

Fast Words

Can you SAY this sentence three times fast? Try it!

Five fine vines are mine.

Now WRITE your own sentence. Use these words or other long **i** words. Then SAY the sentence three times fast!

| piled | tiles | Pete | wide |

Criss Cross

READ the clues. FILL IN the long **e** and **i** words in the boxes.

bike	kite	pipe	time	Pete	dime	bite	nine

Across

2. Ten cents

3. Water goes through this to get

   to your bathtub

4. It comes before ten.

5. A clock tells you the _____.

6. A short word for *bicycle*

Down

1. This flies up in the sky.

3. A nickname for Peter

6. When you eat, you take a big _____.

Slide Words

Let's make words that have a long **o** sound. DRAW a line between each picture and the ending that matches. Then WRITE the first letter of each word.

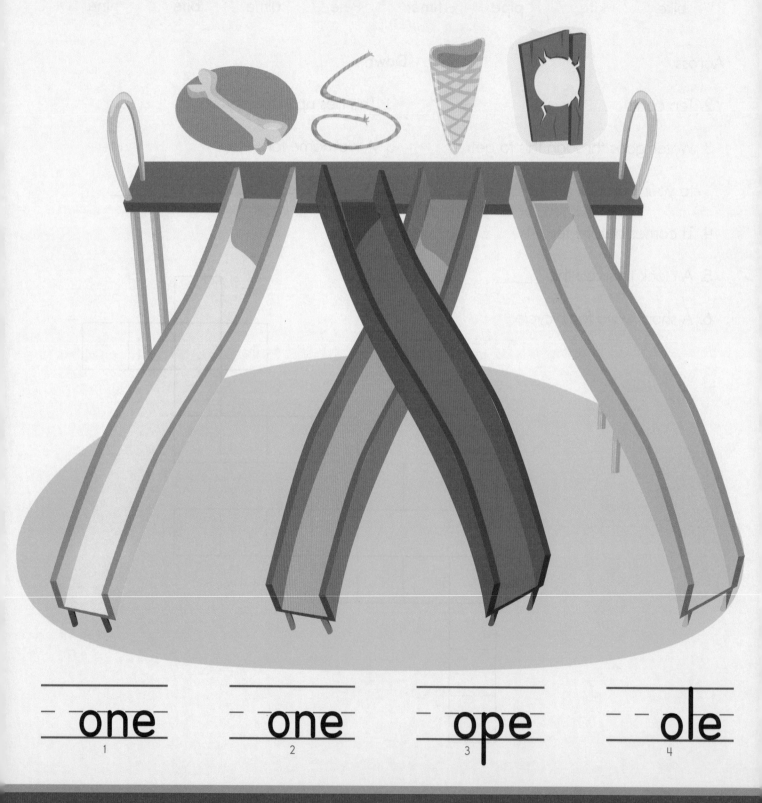

one
1

one
2

ope
3

ole
4

Fast Words

Can you SAY this sentence three times fast? Try it!

The cute duke rode and dozed.

Now WRITE your own sentence. Use these words or other long **o** or long **u** words. Then SAY the sentence three times fast!

holes   poles   homes   in   poke

Spell Long O and U

Letter Liftoff

FILL IN the vowel for each long **o** or long **u** word.

h __ le
1

c __ ne
2

r __ pe
3

d __ ke
4

b __ ne
5

Riddle Me This!

UNSCRAMBLE the words in the riddle.

Q: Why did the kude put

———————

— — — — — — —

his neco on a erpo?

———————   ———————

— — — — — —   — — — — —

———————   ———————

A: He wanted to hang onto it!

Spell Opposites

Opposites Are Everywhere!

FILL IN the word that goes with each picture.

fast or slow?

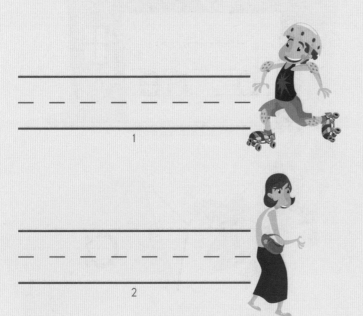

_____
- - - - - - - - - - - - - - - -
1

_____
- - - - - - - - - - - - - - - -
2

big or little?

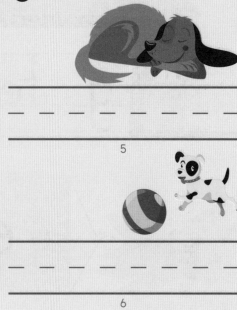

_____
- - - - - - - - - - - - - - - -
5

_____
- - - - - - - - - - - - - - - -
6

hot or cold?

_____
- - - - - - - - - - - - - - - -
3

_____
- - - - - - - - - - - - - - - -
4

short or tall?

_____
- - - - - - - - - - - - - - - -
7

_____
- - - - - - - - - - - - - - - -
8

Perfect Landing

DRAW a line between each word and the missing vowel. WRITE the vowel in the space.

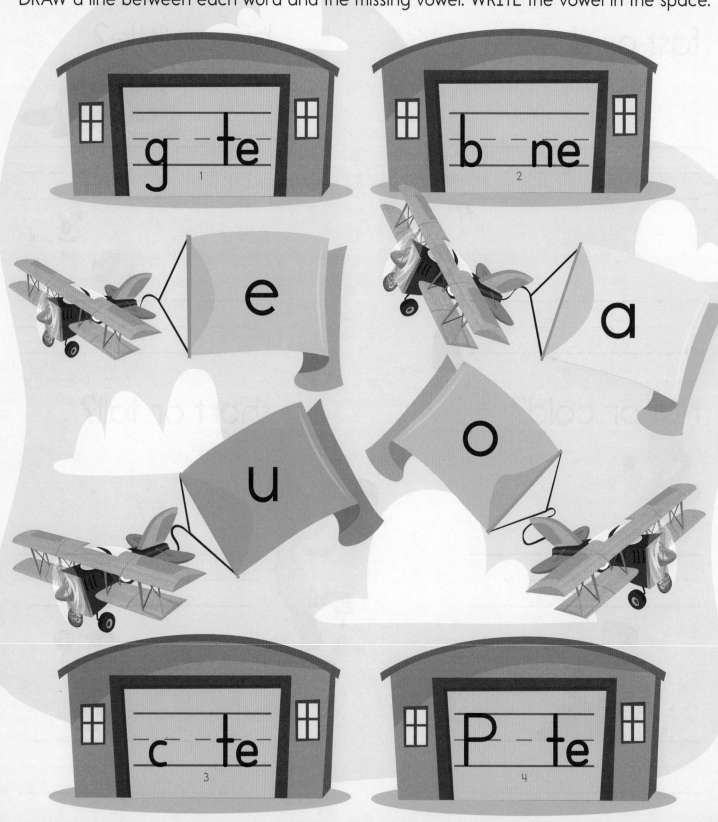

g __ te   1

b __ ne   2

e

a

u

o

c __ te   3

P __ te   4

How Does It End?

The ends of these words got chopped off. DRAW a line between the beginning and end of each word.

k   ate

v   et

f   one

w   ig

c   ox

g   ite

WRITE the words here.

_____   _____   _____

_____   _____   _____

Alphabet Soup

Use the letters in the soup to WRITE the words to match the pictures. CROSS OUT each letter in the soup after you use it.

Bubble Pop

LOOK at the words in the bubbles. CROSS OUT the words that are misspelled.

dook

pol

Pete

pole

lake

byke

duke

lak

Pett

bike

Fix It!

Which letters are missing from the signs? WRITE the correct word under each store.

tes

kes

_____

_____

1

2

nes

kes

_____

_____

3

4

Word Hunt

CIRCLE the **opposite** words in the grid. WRITE each word as you circle it. When you circle a word, CROSS OUT the word in the box. Words go across and down.

| big | small | slow | fast | under | over | tall | short | hot | cold |

```
s  i  l  e  u  b  f  g  c  o  l  d
h  b  t  o  n  x  s  m  a  l  l  v
o  i  a  v  d  e  l  o  f  a  s  t
r  g  l  e  e  h  o  t  w  j  o  h
t  a  l  r  r  n  w  h  x  s  v  t
```

"C" or "K"?

Slide Words

Let's make words that have the letters "c" and "k." DRAW a line between each picture and the ending that matches. Then WRITE the first letter of each word.

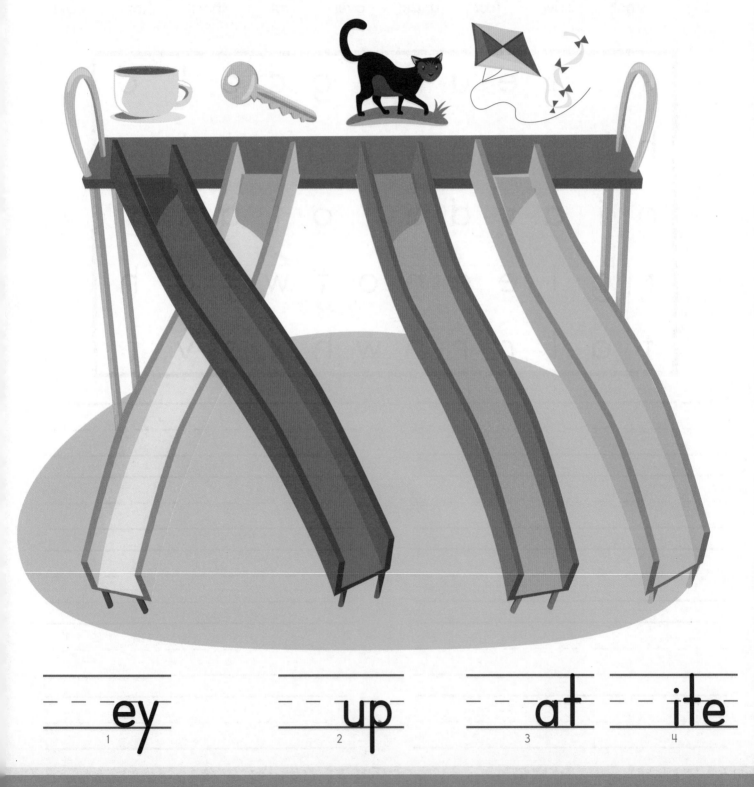

ey
1

up
2

at
3

ite
4

Letter Liftoff

FILL IN the letter "c" or "k" in each space.

bi _ e
1

_ _ ave
2

_ ite
3

_ one
4

_ ake
5

Riddle Me This!

UNSCRAMBLE the words to read the riddle.

Q: Why did the ogd put two dils

_____   _____
— — — — — —   — — — — — —
_____   _____

on his edb?

_____
— — — — —
_____

A: He wanted to sleep under the covers!

Fast Words

Can you SAY this sentence three times fast? Try it!

The bug dug big dog bones.

Now WRITE your own sentence. Use these words or other "b" or "d" words. Then SAY the sentence three times fast!

| buns | bad | baked | Deb |

Travel Tags

Let's make words that have the letters "b" and "p." Then WRITE the words in the tags.

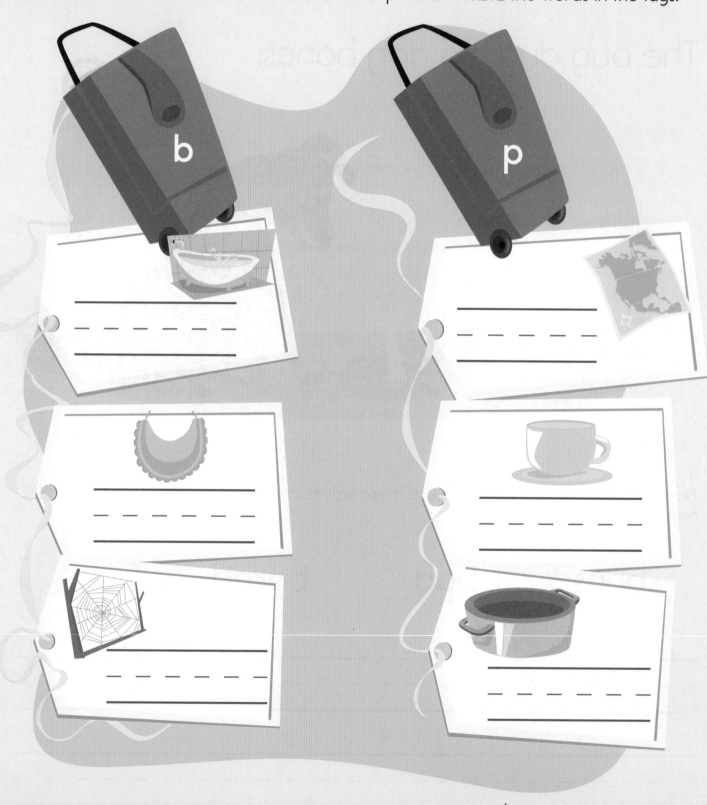

Letter Liftoff

FILL IN the letter "b" or "p" in each space.

ta_e
1

__ike
2

pi_e
3

ro_e
4

_one
5

"S" or "Z"?

Around We Go!

CIRCLE the things that are spelled with the letter "s."

WRITE the words with "s" on the lines.

_____   _____   _____

_ _ _ _ _ _ _ _ _ _ _ _   _ _ _ _ _ _ _ _ _ _ _ _   _ _ _ _ _ _ _ _ _ _ _ _

_____

Criss Cross

READ the clues. FILL IN the words with "s" or "z" in the boxes.

| doze | hose | maze | nose | rose | size |

Across

4. What _____ shoe do you wear?

5. You can use a _____ to water

the flowers.

6. When you take a nap, you _____.

Down

1. A flower that smells nice

2. You can get lost in this.

3. You use this to smell.

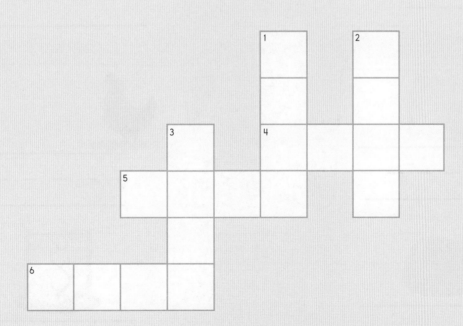

Travel Tags

Let's make words that have the letters "m" and "n." Then WRITE the words in the tags.

Letter Liftoff

FILL IN the letter "v" or "w" in each space.

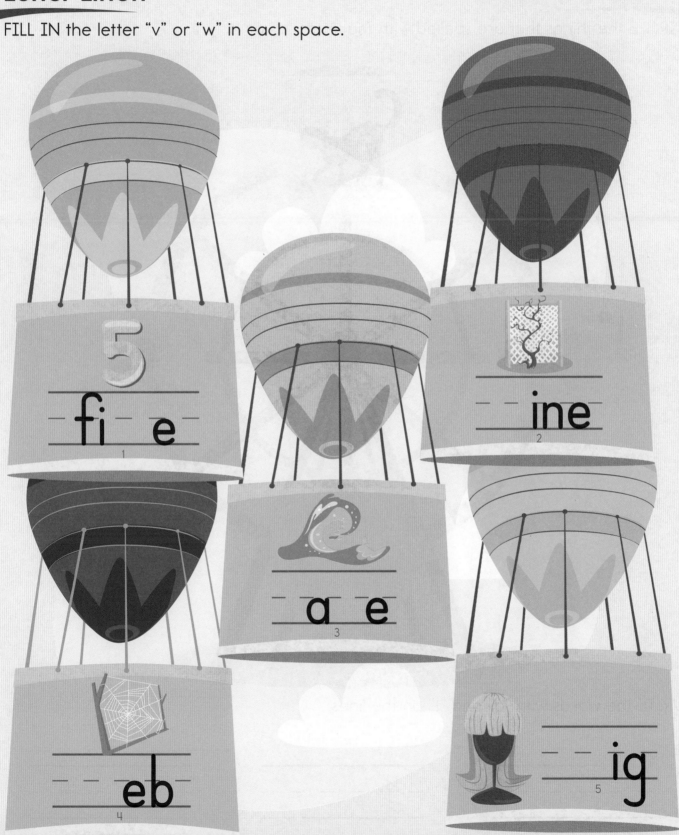

fi _ e
1

_ ine
2

_ a _ e
3

_ eb
4

_ ig
5

Around We Go!

CIRCLE the things that are spelled with the letter "d" or "t."

WRITE the words with "d" and "t" on the lines.

_____   _____   _____

- - - - - - - -   - - - - - - - -   - - - - - - - -

_____   _____   _____

Travel Tags

Let's make words that have the letters "d" and "t." Then WRITE the words in the tags.

Spell with Double Letters

Slide Words

Let's make words that have double letters at the end. DRAW a line between each picture and the ending that matches. Then WRITE the first letter of each word.

___ ell
1

___ oll
2

___ gg
3

___ iss
4

Fast Words

Can you SAY this sentence three times fast? Try it!

The big bell fell on Bill.

Now WRITE your own sentence. Use these words or other words with double letters. Then SAY the sentence three times fast!

dolls	dull	less	sell

_____

- -

_____

- -

_____

Spell Action Words

What's Happening?

FILL IN the **action** word that goes with each picture.

play or nap?

_____

- - - - - - - - -

_____

1

_____

- - - - - - - - -

_____

2

jump or stop?

_____

- - - - - - - - -

_____

5

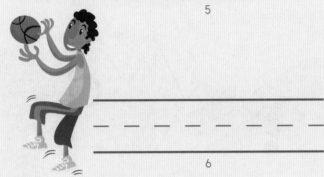

_____

- - - - - - - - -

_____

6

walk or skate?

_____

- - - - - - - - -

_____

3

_____

- - - - - - - - -

_____

4

eat or talk?

_____

- - - - - - - - -

_____

7

_____

- - - - - - - - -

_____

8

Perfect Landing

DRAW a line between each word and the missing letter. WRITE the letter in the space.

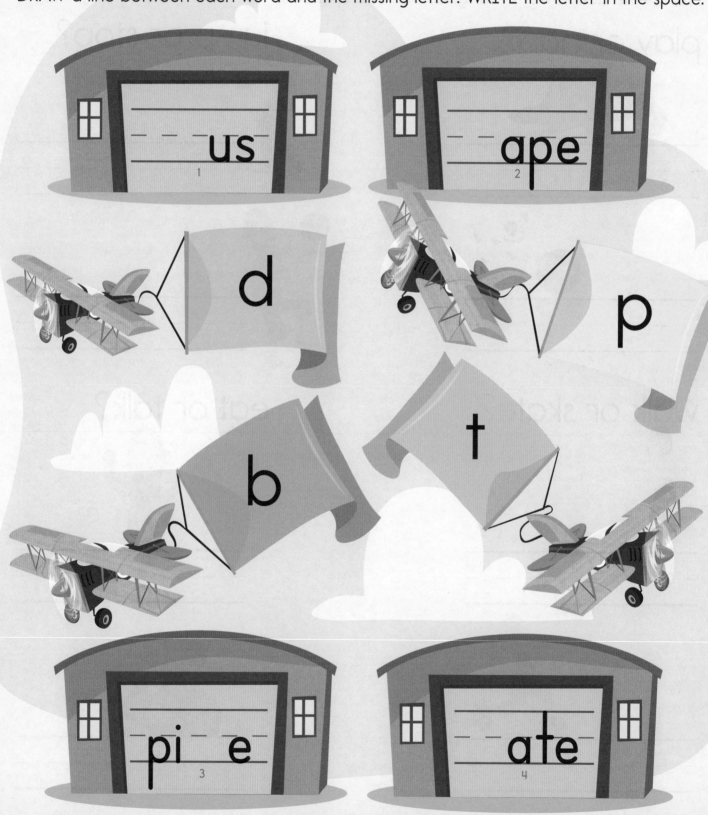

Bubble Pop

LOOK at the words in the bubbles. CROSS OUT the words that are misspelled.

maze

kite

kide

kake

map

cake

mase

mab

nose

noze

Fix It!

CHANGE or ADD the letters to fix the signs. WRITE the correct word under each store.

Dols

Bess

_ _ _ _ _ _ _ _
1

_ _ _ _ _ _ _ _
2

Egs

Wulls

_ _ _ _ _ _ _ _
3

_ _ _ _ _ _ _ _
4

Bubble Pop

LOOK at the **action** words in the bubbles. CROSS OUT the words that are misspelled.

jumb

eat

scate

talk

eet

play

jump

tak

blay

skate

Spell with "-Ed" Endings

Slide Words

To make most action words happen in the past, add "-ed." DRAW a line between each picture and the ending that matches. Then WRITE the beginning of each word.

HINT: If a word has a short vowel sound, double the last letter before adding "-ed."
stop → stopped

play   hug   walk   hop

hug**ged**   play**ed**   walk **ed**   hop**ped**

1   2   3   4

Letter Liftoff

FILL IN the ending for each word to make it past tense. If a word has a short vowel sound, be sure to double the last letter before adding "-ed."

HINT: If a word has an "e" at the end, drop the "e" before adding "-ed."

wave
1

hop
2

talk
3

doze
4

hug
5

Spell with "-Ed" Endings

Travel Tags

Let's make more words past tense. DRAW a line from each suitcase to the tag that matches. Then FILL IN the missing endings.

-ed

drop the "e"

play

skate

wave

walk

How Does It End?

The "-ed" endings of these words got chopped off! DRAW a line between the beginning and end of each word. Then WRITE the words in the boxes.

hug	ded
bake	ped
stop	ed
talk	d
nod	ged
miss	‾ed

Spell with "-Ing" Endings

Letter Liftoff

Sometimes action words end with "-ing." FILL IN the "ing" ending for these words.

eat ___ 1

play ___ 2

walk ___ 3

talk ___ 4

How Does It End?

DRAW a line between the beginning and end of each word. WRITE the words in the boxes.

HINT: If a word has a short vowel sound, double the last letter before adding "-ing": hop → hopping.

run   ning

cut   ping

sit   ting

nap   bing

rub   ping

hop   ting

Tricky Endings

Try this trick for making words that end with "-ing." When a word ends with "e," take off the "e" and add "-ing": **ride → riding**

hide ➡

1

rake ➡

2

doze ➡

3

bite ➡

4

tune ➡️ _____
5

skate ➡️ _____
6

dive ➡️ _____
7

poke ➡️ _____
8

How Do You Do It?

A word that tells **how** someone does something ends with "-ly." WRITE an "-ly" word on each sign so people know what to do!

Be safe in the water.

Swim _____

Be nice when you talk.

Talk _____

Go for a slow ride.

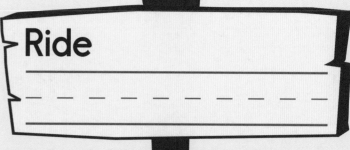

Ride _____

Letter Liftoff

FILL IN the beginning letter of each animal word.

__ nake
1

__ rog
2

__ ion
3

__ ouse
4

__ oat
5

Soccer Star

DRAW a line between each picture and the end of the word to make it past tense.
WRITE the words in the nets.

Fix It!

One word on each sign is misspelled. WRITE the correct word under each store.

Log Cuting

Cake Bakeng

1

2

Horse Rideing

Bike Fixng

3

4

Bubble Pop

LOOK at the words in the bubbles. CROSS OUT the words that are misspelled.

badly

nicley

safly

nicely

slowly

badley

wiseley

wisely

safely

slowely

Word Hunt

CIRCLE the **animal words** in the grid. WRITE each word as you circle it. When you circle a word, CROSS OUT the word in the box. Words go across and down.

| cow | horse | frog | bird | goat | mouse | snake | fish | lion | cat |

```
l  i  o  n  n  m  s  h  a  l  s  v
p  u  f  m  b  o  g  o  a  t  n  f
g  t  r  l  i  u  o  r  c  j  a  i
x  c  o  w  r  s  p  s  a  d  k  s
o  l  g  s  d  e  r  e  t  i  e  h
```

Spell Plurals

Letter Liftoff

Plural means "more than one." When a word tells about more than one thing, add an "-s": **hat → hats**

WRITE plural words. ADD an "-s" to each word.

bird
1

kite
2

egg
3

bone
4

cat
5

Tricky Endings

If a word ends with "x" or "s," to make it plural, add "-es": **box → boxes**

Try it! WRITE plural words by adding "-es" to these words.

bus →

1

fox →

2

kiss →

3

mess →

4

box →

5

What Do You See at the Party?

What do you see at Kate's birthday party? FILL IN the blanks using **plural** words.

| cakes | kisses | hats | boxes | cups | buses |

1. There are two pink birthday _____ on the table.

2. The kids are wearing _____ with dots on them.

3. The _____ have presents inside.

4. The blue _____ are on the table too.

5. Tim is playing with yellow toy _____ .

6. Kate's mother and father are giving her _____ _____ .

People Words with "-Er"

Getting to Know You

Some words that end with "-er" tell about people. WRITE the word that matches each person.

eater	jumper	kisser	talker	walker

_____

_____

1

_____

_____

2

_____

_____

3

_____

_____

4

_____

_____

5

What Do You Do?

WRITE "-er" words that tell about these people.

HINT: When a word ends with an "e," drop the "e" before adding "-er."

1. If you **bake** a cake, you are a _____.

2. If you work in a **mine**, you are a _____.

3. If you ride your **bike**, you are a _____.

4. If you like to **skate**, you are a _____.

5. If you **rope** cows, you are a _____.

6. If you **dive** into the water, you are a _____.

How Does It End?

DRAW a line between each word and its "-er" ending. WRITE the words in the boxes.

HINT: When a word has a short vowel sound, double the last letter before adding "-er."

swim   ger

hop   per

win   ner

sit   mer

hug   ter

nap   per

Criss Cross

READ the clues. FILL IN the people words in the boxes.

teacher   baker   eater   talker   diver   digger   skater

Across

2. A person who bakes cakes

3. He likes to skate.

4. A person who digs

6. Someone who teaches

Down

1. A person who talks and talks

4. She dives into the pool.

5. Someone who eats

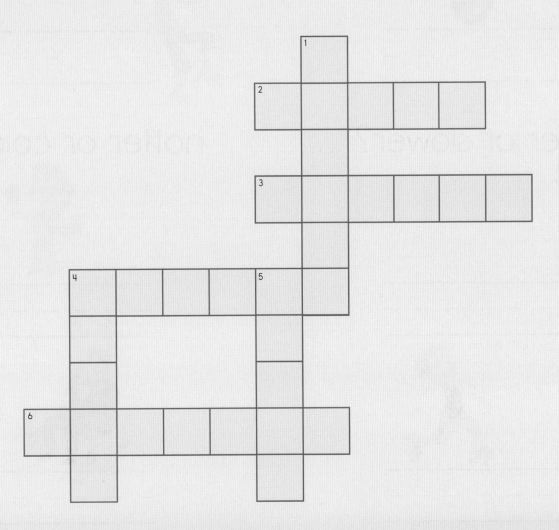

Look and Compare

Add "-er" at the end of describing words to compare two things. WRITE the "-er" word that tells about each person or animal.

bigger or smaller?

_____

- - - - - - - - - - - - - - -

_____
1

_____

- - - - - - - - - - - - - - -

_____
2

shorter or taller?

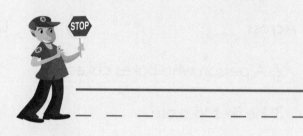

_____

- - - - - - - - - - - - - - -

_____
5

_____

- - - - - - - - - - - - - - -

_____
6

faster or slower?

_____

- - - - - - - - - - - - - - -

_____
3

_____

- - - - - - - - - - - - - - -

_____
4

hotter or colder?

_____

- - - - - - - - - - - - - - -

_____
7

_____

- - - - - - - - - - - - - - -

_____
8

Compare the Racers

Add "-est" at the end of a describing word when you compare more than two things.
FILL IN the "-est" word that tells about each car in the race.

slowest   fastest   biggest   smallest   hottest   wettest

More People

Letter Liftoff

Who are these people? FILL IN the first letter of each word.

__ __ aby
1

__ __ irl
2

__ __ oy
3

__ __ an
4

__ __ ady
5

Criss Cross

READ the clues. FILL IN the people words in the boxes.

mother   boys   sister   man   baby   girl   father

Across

2. The opposite of *girls* is _____.

5. Another word for *dad* is _____.

6. Another word for *mom* is _____.

Down

1. A _____ is very little.

3. The opposite of *brother* is _____.

4. A _____ will grow up to be a lady.

6. Your father is a _____.

Fix It!

CHANGE or ADD vowels to fix the signs. WRITE the correct words under each store.

Bik Rydes	Rud Rekes
1	2

Fesh Nots	Dag Bids
3	4

Bubble Pop

LOOK at the words in the bubbles. CROSS OUT the words that are misspelled.

stoped

talkng

rakd

raked

hiding

hideing

slowley

slowly

talking

stopped

Soccer Star

Make a noun plural by adding "-s" or "-es." DRAW a line between each picture and the end of the word. WRITE the plural words in the nets.

Word Hunt

CIRCLE the **people** words in the grid. WRITE each word as you circle it. When you circle a word, CROSS OUT the word in the box. Words go across and down.

mother	boy	baby	skater	teacher
father	girl	swimmer	baker	talker

```
t e a c h e r b a b y g
b i f a t h e r k a h i
s k a t e r t a l k e r
m b o y t m o t h e r l
h g c s w i m m e r t h
```

Answers

Page 2
1. ram
2. cat
3. map
4. fan

Page 3
Suggestion: The man and the ram ran.

Page 4
1. ram
2. rat
3. hat
4. bat

Page 5

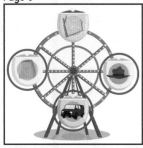

hat, van, bag

Page 6
1. The ram eats a **yam**.
2. The fan cools the **man**.
3. The hat is on the **cat**.

Page 7
Suggestions: bag, bat, cat, gab, gas, rag, rat, sag, sat, tab, tag

Page 8
1. pen
2. leg
3. bed
4. vet

Page 9
1. hen
2. bed
3. ten
4. pen
5. net

Page 10

web, hen, pen

Page 11
Suggestion: Red beds have red legs.

Page 12
1. The wet pet saw the **vet**.
2. The hen has a **pen**.
3. The bed was **red**.

Page 13
Suggestions: bed, bet, den, jet, men, met, net, ten, Jeb, Jed, Deb, Ted, Ned

Pages 14-15
1. one
2. two
3. three
4. four
5. five
6. six
7. seven
8. eight

Page 16
1. net
2. hat
3. jet
4. van

Page 17
a: bat, cat, fan
e: bed, hen, vet

Page 18
1. one
2. four
3. six
4. ten

Page 19

Page 20
1. six
2. wig
3. bib
4. pin

Page 21

wig, bin, pig

Page 22
Suggestion: Pigs dig big kids.

Page 23
1. dig
2. pig
3. pin
4. bin

Page 24
1. The pig lost her **wig**.
2. My pin fell in the **bin**.
3. "Help me dig," said the **pig**.

Page 25
Suggestions: big, bin, bit, nib, nip, nit, pig, pin, pit, tip, tin, wig, win, wit

Page 26
1. dog
2. box
3. pot
4. mop

Page 27
1. pot
2. dot
3. dog
4. log

Page 28
1. The dog jumps on a **log**.
2. The box is on top of the **fox**.
3. Can you hop over the **top**?

Page 29
Suggestion: The fox mops a box.

Page 30
Suggestions: dog, dot, god, got, hog, hop, hot, mop, pod, pot, top, Tom

Page 31
Q. What **dog** pops out of a **pot** that is **hot**?

Page 32
1. cup
2. bus
3. sun
4. tub

Page 33
1. The cub jumped in the **tub**.
2. The pup found a **cup**.
3. The bug hid under the **rug**.

Page 34

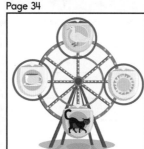

cup, duck, sun

Page 35
Q: Why did the **bug** drive his **bus** into the **tub**?
Note: *bus* or *sub* works, but *bus* matches the picture.

Page 36
Suggestions: bug, bum, bun, bus, gum, gun, Gus, mug, rub, rug, run, sub, sum, sun

Page 37
ACROSS   DOWN
1. hut   2. tub
3. bus   4. sun
5. bug   5. but
7. nut   6. gum
8. mud

Pages 38-39
1. green
2. blue
3. brown
4. red
5. yellow
6. white
7. purple
8. orange

Page 40
1. pin
2. box
3. mud
4. mom

Page 41
1. pig
2. fox
3. tub
4. bus

Page 42
1. Hets → Hats
2. Bids → Beds
3. Rogs → Rugs
4. Mups → Mops

Page 43
Misspelled Words: blu, purpel, yello, gren, orang

Page 44
1. cake
2. gate
3. wave
4. cane

Page 45
1. wave
2. cave
3. cane
4. cape

Page 46

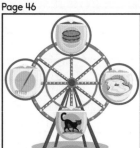

rake, cake, lake

Page 47
Suggestion: Safe waves save lakes.

Page 48
1. vine
2. Pete
3. kite
4. bike

Answers

Page 49
1. Pete
2. pipe
3. bike
4. kite
5. nine

Page 50
Suggestion: Pete piled wide tiles.

Page 51

ACROSS	DOWN
2. dime	1. kite
3. pipe	3. Pete
4. nine	6. bite
5. time	
6. bike	

Page 52
1. bone
2. cone
3. rope
4. hole

Page 53
Suggestion: Poles poke holes in homes.

Page 54
1. hole
2. cone
3. rope
4. duke
5. bone

Page 55
Q: Why did the **duke** put his **cone** on a **rope**?

Pages 56-57
1. fast
2. slow
3. cold
4. hot
5. big
6. little
7. tall
8. short

Page 58
1. gate
2. bone
3. cute
4. Pete

Page 59
kite, vet, fox, wig, cone, gate
Note: You can make *fate, fig, fox, wet, wig, gate, get, gone, gig* too, but you'll have leftover beginnings or ends.

Page 60
1. duke
2. gate
3. pipe
4. rope

Page 61
Misspelled Words: dook, pol, byke, Pett, lak

Page 62
1. __tes →Gates
2. __kes →Bikes
3. __nes →Cones
4. __kes →Rakes

Page 63

Page 64
1. key
2. cup
3. cat
4. kite

Page 65
1. bike
2. cave
3. kite
4. cone
5. cake

Page 66
Q: Why did the **dog** put two **lids** on his **bed**?

Page 67
Suggestion: Deb baked bad buns.

Page 68
b: tub, bib, web
p: map, cup, pot

Page 69
1. tape
2. bike
3. pipe
4. rope
5. bone

Page 70

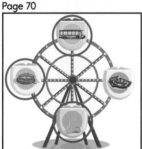

hose, bus, nose

Page 71

ACROSS	DOWN
4. size	1. rose
5. hose	2. maze
6. doze	3. nose

Page 72
m: map, dime, ham
n: nut, hen, vine

Page 73
Suggestion: Mike named nine mice.

Page 74
1. van
2. wig
3. vet
4. web

Page 75
1. five
2. vine
3. wave
4. web
5. wig

Page 76

bed, cat, top

Page 77
d: dive, dime, bed
t: tape, kite, net

Page 78
1. bell
2. doll
3. egg
4. kiss

Page 79
Suggestion: Dull dolls sell less.

Pages 80-81
1. nap
2. play
3. walk
4. skate
5. stop
6. jump
7. eat
8. talk

Page 82
1. **b**us
2. **t**ape
3. pi**p**e
4. **d**ate

Page 83
Misspelled Words: mase, noze, kake, mab, kide

Page 84
1. Dols →Dolls
2. Bess →Bells
3. Egs →Eggs
4. Wulls →Wells

Page 85
Misspelled Words: scate , tak, eet, jumb, blay

Page 86
1. hugged
2. played
3. walked
4. hopped

Page 87
1. waved
2. hopped
3. talked
4. dozed
5. hugged

Page 88
-ed: played, walked
Drop the "e": waved skated

Page 89
hugged, baked, stopped, talked, nodded, missed

Page 90
1. eating
2. playing
3. walking
4. talking

Page 91
running, cutting, sitting, napping, rubbing, hopping

Pages 92-93
1. hide →hiding
2. rake →raking
3. doze →dozing
4. bite →biting
5. tune →tuning
6. skate →skating
7. dive →diving
8. poke →poking

Page 94
1. Swim **Safely**
2. Talk **Nicely**
3. Ride **Slowly**

Page 95
Suggestion: Fly kites nicely and wisely.

Page 96
1. cow
2. horse
3. bird
4. fish

Page 97
1. snake
2. frog
3. lion
4. mouse
5. goat

Page 98
-d: waved, skated, dozed
-ed: walked, kissed, played

Page 99
1. Cuting →Cutting
2. Bakeng →Baking
3. Rideing →Riding
4. Fixng →Fixing

Page 100
Misspelled Words: slowely, safly, wiseley, badley, nicley

Page 101

Answers

Page 102
1. birds
2. kites
3. eggs
4. bones
5. cats

Page 103
1. buses
2. foxes
3. kisses
4. messes
5. boxes

Pages 104-105
1. cakes
2. hats
3. boxes
4. cups
5. buses
6. kisses

Page 106
1. eater
2. jumper
3. walker
4. kisser
5. talker

Page 107
1. baker
2. miner
3. biker
4. skater
5. roper
6. diver

Page 108
swimmer, hopper, winner, sitter, hugger, napper

Page 109
ACROSS
2. baker
3. skater
4. digger
6. teacher

DOWN
1. talker
4. diver
5. eater

Page 110
1. bigger
2. smaller
3. slower
4. faster
5. shorter
6. taller
7. colder
8. hotter

Page 111
1. biggest
2. slowest
3. smallest
4. hottest
5. wettest
6. fastest

Page 112
1. baby
2. girl
3. boy
4. man
5. lady

Page 113
ACROSS
2. boys
5. father
6. mother

DOWN
1. baby
3. sister
4. girl
6. man

Page 114
1. Bik Rydes →Bike Rides
2. Rud Rekes →Red Rakes
3. Fesh Nots →Fish Nets
4. Dag Bids →Dog Beds

Page 115
1. bed
2. bite
3. tape
4. duke

Page 116
1. cone
2. rake
3. hose
4. maze

Page 117
Misspelled words: hideing, stoped, slowley, rakd, talkng

Page 118
-s: birds, eggs, cows
-es: buses, foxes, boxes

Page 119

1st Grade
Vocabulary Puzzles

Contents

Read and Trace

READ the words and TRACE them. Do you know what they mean?

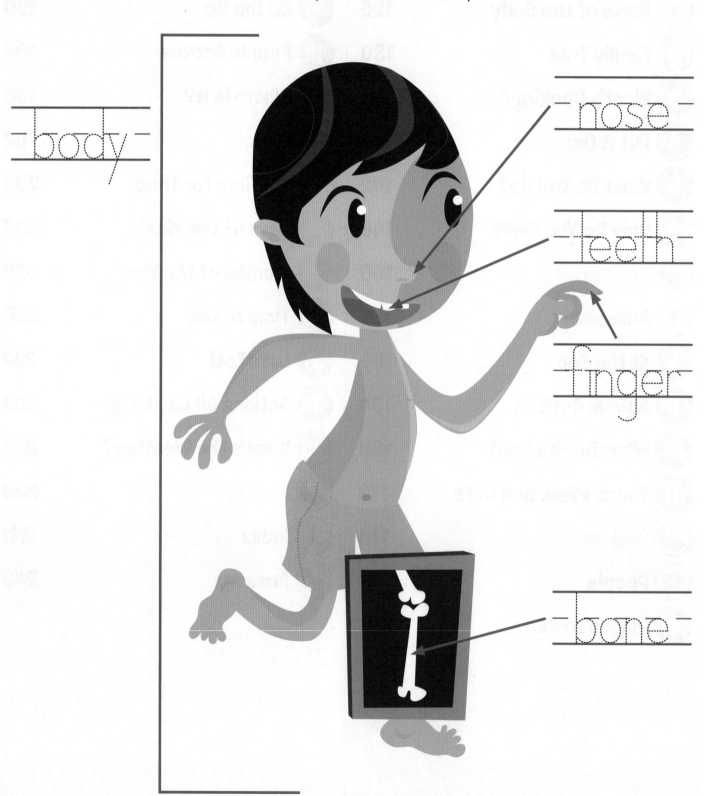

body

nose

teeth

finger

bone

Picture Pointers

WRITE the word for each picture clue in the grid.

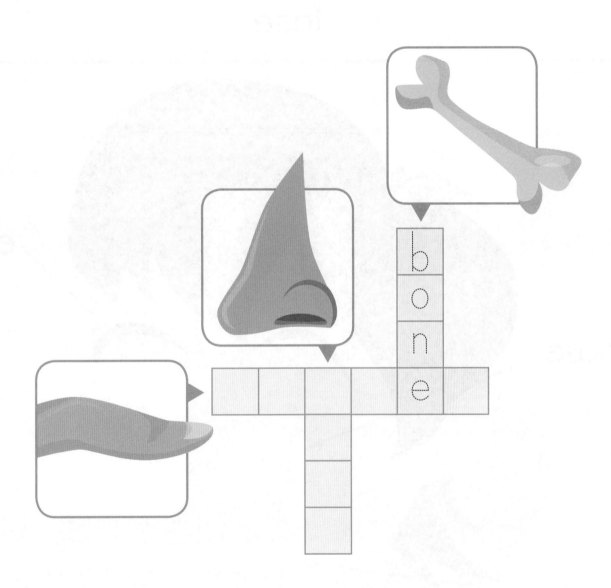

Draw It

Help finish the picture! DRAW parts of the face to match the words.

face

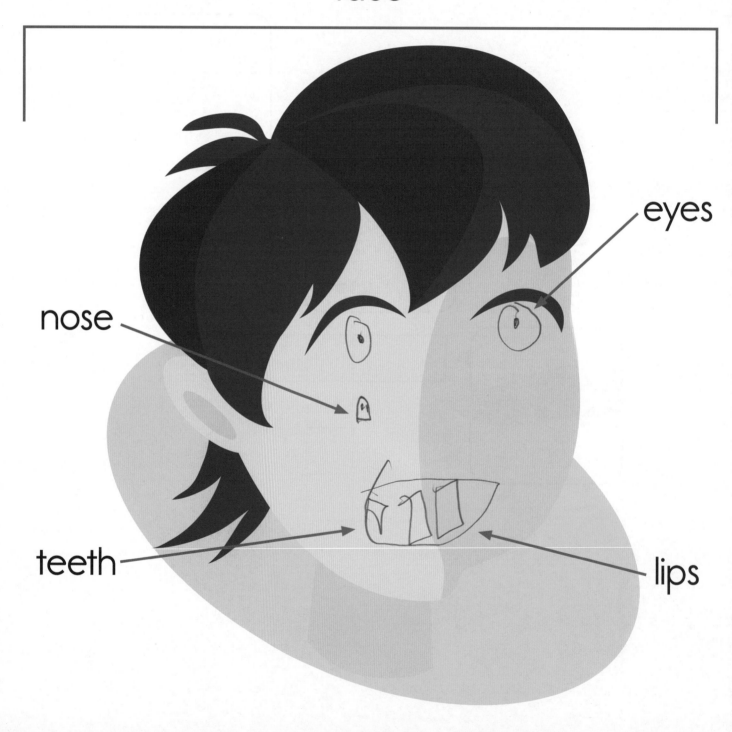

eyes

nose

teeth

lips

Maze Crazy!

DRAW a line through the words for **body parts** to get to the boy. START at the yellow arrow.

Read and Trace

READ the words and TRACE them. Do you know what they mean?

family

father

mother

daughter

son

Match the Meaning

DRAW a line to match the word with its picture.

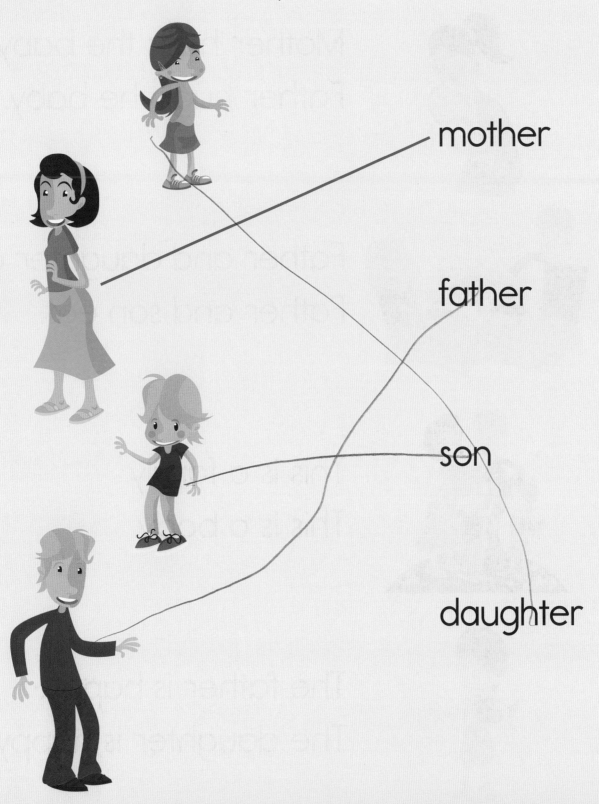

mother

father

son

daughter

Right or Wrong?

UNDERLINE the sentence that matches the picture.

1.

Mother hugs the baby.

Father hugs the baby.

2.

Father and daughter eat.

Father and son eat.

3.

This is a family.

This is a body.

4.

The father is happy.

The daughter is happy.

Word Pictures

COLOR the spaces that show words for FAMILY.

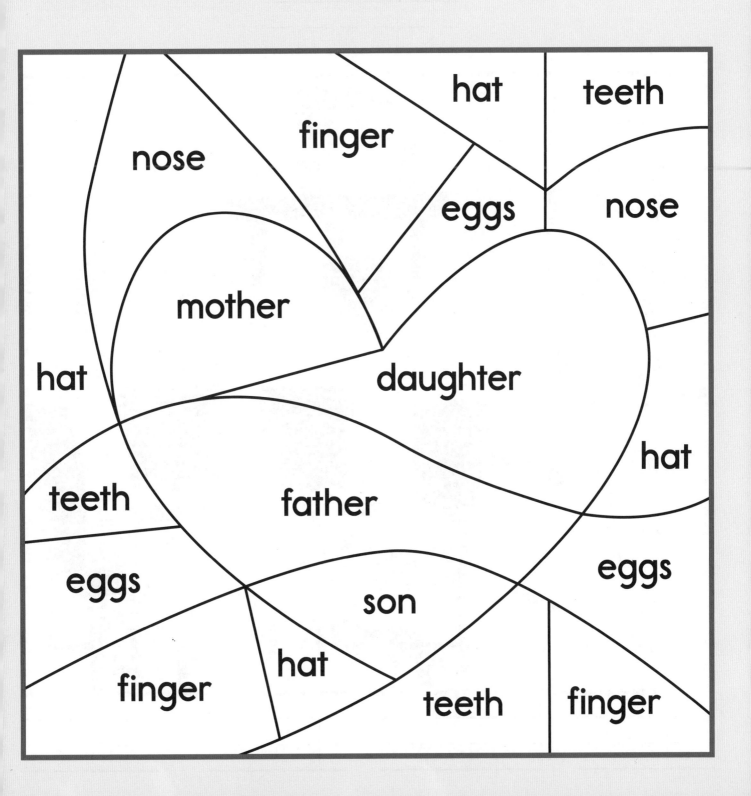

What's Cooking?

Read and Trace

READ the words and TRACE them. Do you know what they mean?

kitchen

stove   spoon   knife   fork

Cross Out

CROSS OUT things that **don't** go in the **kitchen**.

Put It On!

Read and Trace

READ the words and TRACE them. Do you know what they mean?

clothes

coat

button

shirt

jeans

Picture Pointers

WRITE the word for each picture clue in the grid.

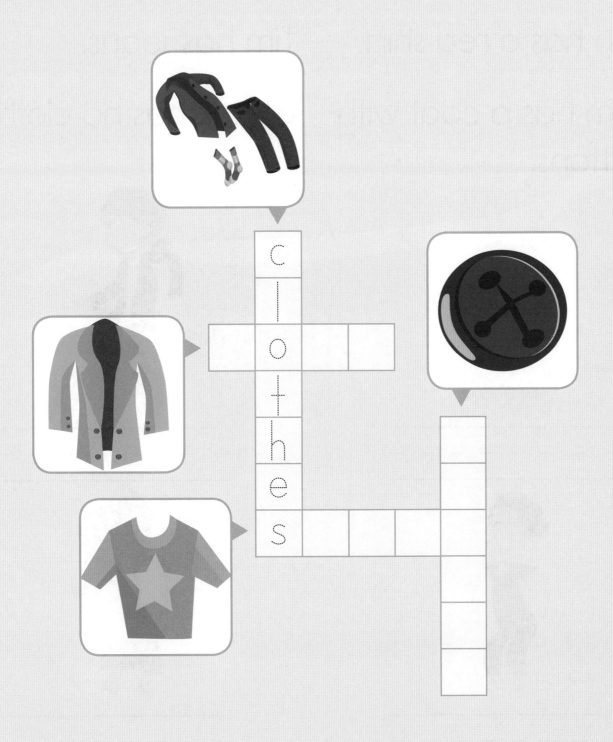

Put It On!

Find the Friend

READ the clues. Then WRITE the friend's name under each picture.

Ken has a red shirt.　　Tim has jeans.

Pam has a coat with　　Chuck has no clothes!
buttons.

- - - - - - - -

- - - - - - - -

Hide and Seek

CIRCLE the clothes in the picture.

What Do You Do?

Read and Trace

Things you do are called **actions**. TRACE the action words in the sentences below.

You ‾wear‾ clothes.

You ‾wash‾ dishes.

You ‾cook‾ at the stove.

You ‾drink‾ juice.

You ‾visit‾ friends.

Match the Meaning

The pictures below are in need of action! DRAW a line to match the action word with the right picture.

wear

wash

cook

drink

visit

What Do You Do?

Circle It

CIRCLE the words that are actions.

1. eat   run   stove   red

2. baby   play   wash   cake

3. wear   leg   green   hug

4. visit   nose   cook   kitchen

Right or Wrong?

UNDERLINE the sentence that matches the picture.

1.

I drink my hands.

I wash my hands.

2.

I visit my granny.

I cook my granny.

3.

I wear my mittens.

I wash my mittens.

4.

Bob visits juice.

Bob drinks juice.

Read and Trace

READ the words about feelings and TRACE them. Do you know what they mean?

You are _hungry_ when you want to eat.

You are _thirsty_ when you want to drink.

You are _unhappy_ when you feel sad.

You are _angry_ when you feel mad.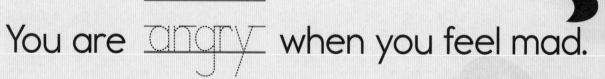

Are you _afraid_ of the dark?

Draw It!

Help finish the picture! DRAW parts of the face to match the words.

HINT: Is a girl who is unhappy smiling or frowning?

unhappy

angry

afraid

happy

How Do You Feel?

Circle It

CIRCLE the words that are feelings.

1. wash   sad   daughter   angry

2. shirt   clothes   afraid   happy

3. drink   fork   knife   thirsty

4. hungry   body   mad   son

Match the Meaning

DRAW a line to match the words that have the same meaning.

afraid   sad

unhappy   scared

angry   nap

drink   mad

sleep   sip

Word Pictures

COLOR the spaces that show words for **clothes**.

Picture Pointers

WRITE the word for each picture clue in the grid.

Circle It

CIRCLE the words that are parts of the body.

1. arm   wash   action   eyes

2. hungry   leg   finger   jeans

3. nose   drink   teeth   son

4. visit   face   spoon   lips

Right or Wrong?

UNDERLINE the sentence that matches the picture.

1.

Father is angry.

Father is afraid.

2.

Jill wears a hat.

Jill washes a hat.

3.

Sam cut his fork

Sam cut his finger.

4.

Mother cooks eggs.

Mother cools eggs.

Maze Crazy!

DRAW a line through the words for **family** to get home. Start at the yellow arrow.

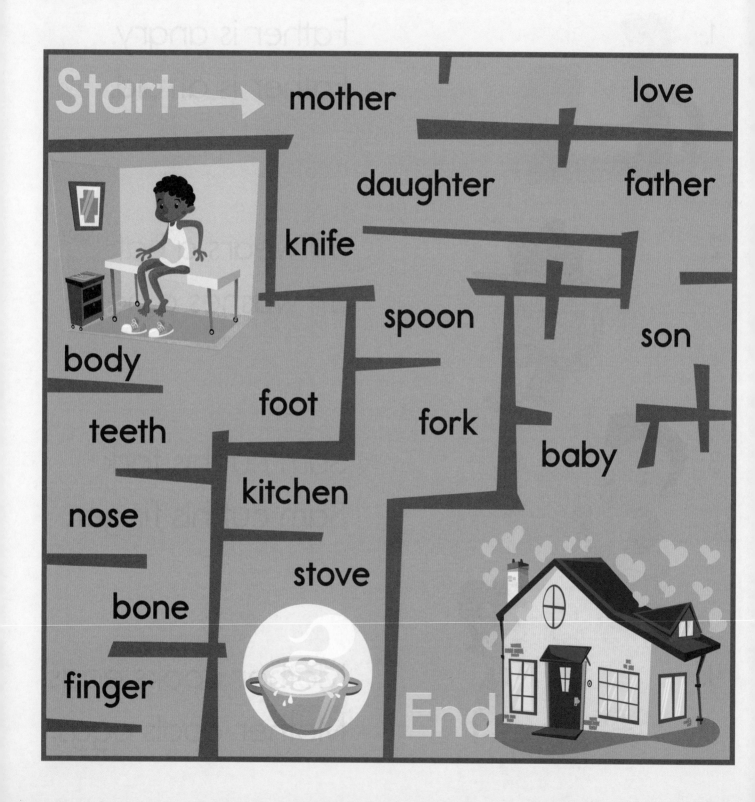

Yes or No?

LOOK at the picture. READ the questions about Pat. CIRCLE YES or NO to answer.

1. Is Pat a daughter?   YES   NO

2. Is Pat cooking?   YES   NO

3. Is Pat angry?   YES   NO

4. Is Pat wearing a coat?   YES   NO

5. Does Pat have hair?   YES   NO

Animals

Read and Trace

READ the words and TRACE them. Do you know what they mean?

Draw It

Help finish the pictures! COLOR or DRAW the pictures to match the sentences.

The leopard is yellow.

The kangaroo is red.

The gorilla wears a hat.

The penguin has a blue belly.

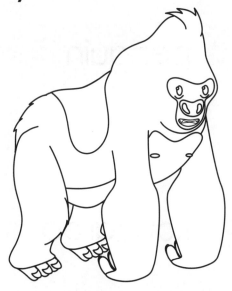

Match the Meaning

DRAW a line to match the word with its picture.

walrus

penguin

kangaroo

gorilla

Word Pictures

COLOR the spaces that show words for **animals**.

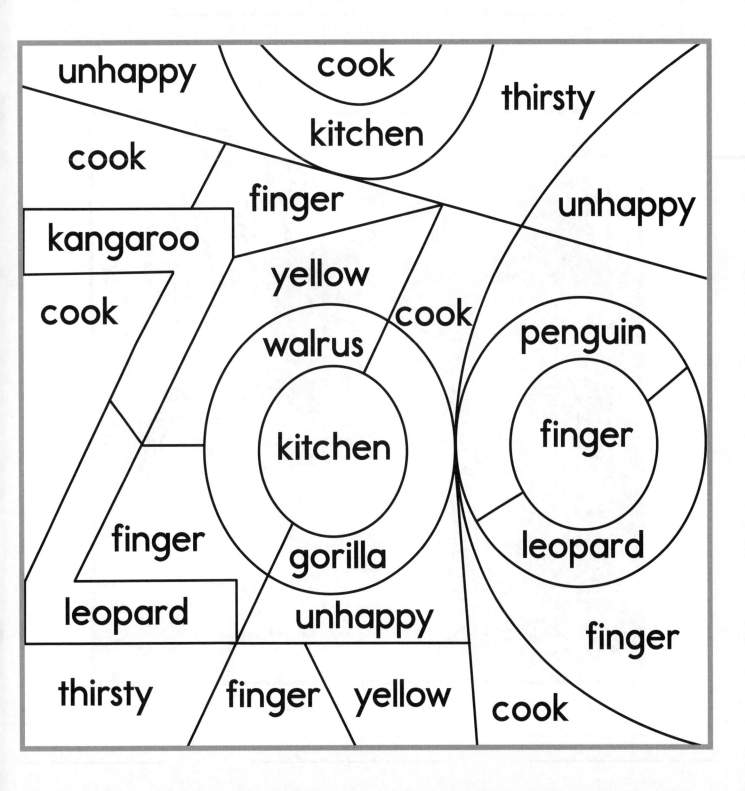

unhappy

cook

thirsty

cook

kitchen

finger

unhappy

kangaroo

yellow

cook

cook

walrus

penguin

kitchen

finger

finger

gorilla

leopard

leopard

unhappy

finger

thirsty

finger

yellow

cook

Read and Trace

READ the words and TRACE them. Do you know what they mean?

cage   balloon

pigeon   skates   pool

Yes or No?

LOOK at the picture. READ the questions about Tara. CIRCLE YES or NO to answer.

1. Does Tara have a balloon?   YES   NO

2. Is Tara in a cage?   YES   NO

3. Is there a walrus on Tara's shirt? YES   NO

4. Is Tara in a pool?   YES   NO

5. Is Tara wearing skates?   YES   NO

Picture Pointers

WRITE the word for each picture clue in the grid.

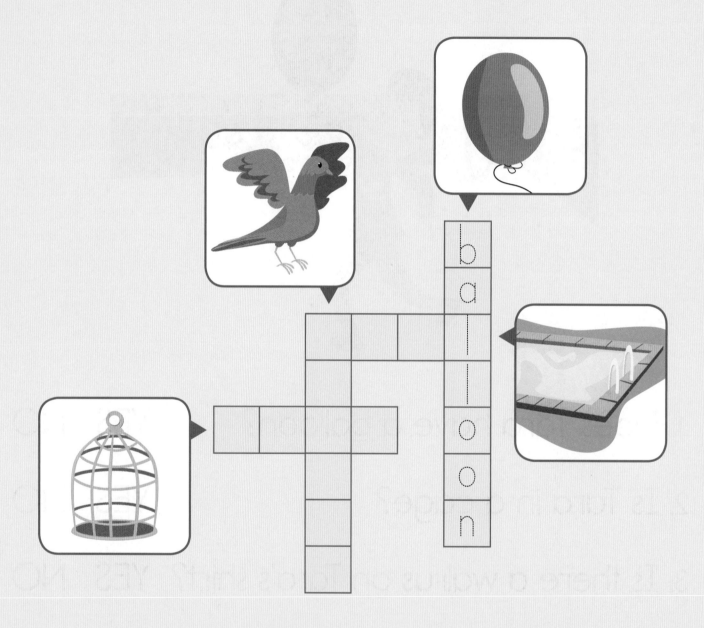

Match the Meaning

CIRCLE the picture that matches the word.

1. sharp

2. dry

3. young

4. colorful

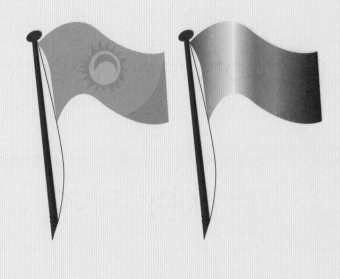

What Do You See?

Blank Out

FINISH each sentence with a word from the word box. CROSS OUT the words as you use them.

| dry | young | sharp | silly | colorful |

1. When I feel _____, I giggle a lot.

2. A knife is very _____.

3. I like to draw _____ pictures.

4. Boots keep your feet _____ in the rain.

5. The baby is too _____ to walk.

Night and Day

Opposites are two words that mean very different things, like *wet* and *dry*.

DRAW a line to match each word under the moon to its opposite under the sun.

wet

unhappy

hot

young

gray

colorful

dry

cold

happy

old

Yours, Mine, and Ours

Read and Trace

If something **belongs** to you, then you own it. READ the words and TRACE them. Do you know what they mean?

HINT: When you use someone's name, you need to use a punctuation mark called an *apostrophe* before the "s."

Who does the balloon _belong_ to?

The balloon is _mine_.

It is _my_ balloon.

The skates are _his_.

The spoon is _hers_.

The puppy is <u>ours</u>.

It is <u>our</u> puppy.

That is Wanda<u>'s</u> chair.

That coat is <u>yours</u>.

It is <u>your</u> coat.

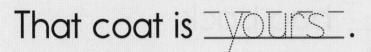

Blank Out

FINISH each sentence with a word from the word box. CROSS OUT the words as you use them.

his	her	mine	ours	yours

1. That toy belongs to me. It is _____.

2. Give this ball to Jake. It is _____.

3. That candy belongs to you. It is _____.

4. Tara wants _____ bag back.

5. We made that picture. It is _____.

Match the Meaning

DRAW a line to match the words that **belong** together.

Lori   mine

me   hers

you   his

him   Lori's

her   ours

us   yours

Circle It

CIRCLE the words that are animals.

1. monkey bone   escape   rat

2. sharp   walrus swing   penguin

3. pigeon finger kitchen kangaroo

4. skates   afraid gorilla leopard

Yes or No?

LOOK at the picture. READ the questions. CIRCLE YES or NO to answer.

1. Does this man look angry?   YES   NO

2. Is this man dry?   YES   NO

3. Does this man wear
   colorful clothes?   YES   NO

4. Is this man cooking?   YES   NO

5. Is this man young?   YES   NO

Review

Maze Crazy!

DRAW a line through the words for **feelings** to get to the smiling girl. Start at the green arrow.

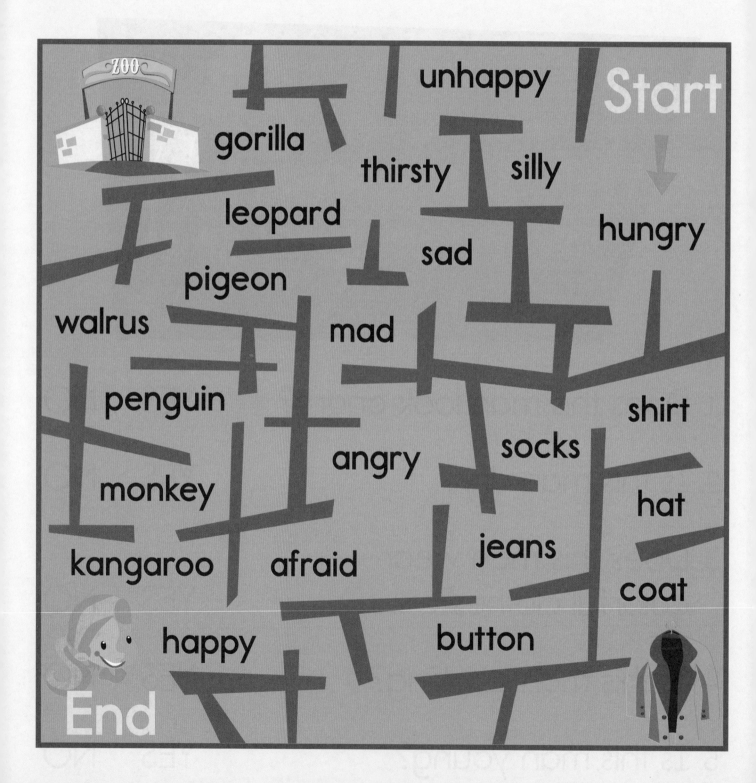

ZOO

unhappy

Start

gorilla

thirsty   silly

leopard

hungry

sad

pigeon

walrus

mad

penguin

shirt

socks

angry

monkey

hat

jeans

kangaroo   afraid

coat

happy

button

End

Blank Out

FINISH each sentence with a word from the word box. CROSS OUT the words as you use them.

afraid   float   belongs   escaped   kitchen

1. We cook our food in the _____.

2. Hold your balloon or it will _____ away.

3. My pet rat _____ from his cage.

4. That is my book. It _____ to me.

5. Eek! I am _____ of bugs.

Right or Wrong?

UNDERLINE the sentence that matches the picture.

1.

   The dog has a balloon.
   The dog has a bone.

2.

   The kid climbs a tree.
   The kid cooks a tree.

3.

   The pigeon is in a cage.
   The penguin is in a cage.

4.

   Jan swings in the yard.
   Jan skates in the yard.

Picture Pointers

WRITE the word for each picture clue in the grid.

People

Read and Trace

READ the words and TRACE them. Do you know what they mean?

mailman   doctor   teacher

policeman   burglar

Hide and Seek

LOOK at the words in the word box. CIRCLE these **people** in the picture. CROSS OUT the words as you find them.

> policeman   mother   mailman   father

Read and Trace

READ the words and TRACE them. Do you know what they mean?

playground bridge building

station market

Picture Pointers

WRITE the word for each picture clue in the grid.

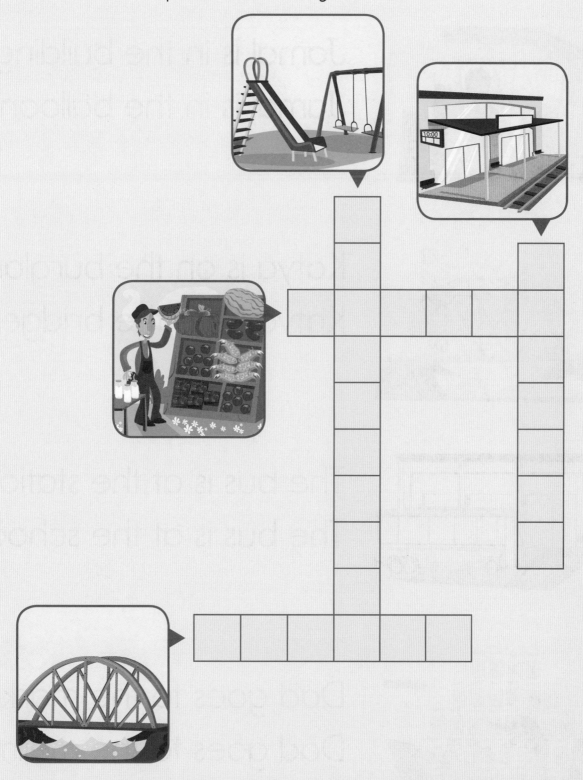

Right or Wrong?

UNDERLINE the sentence that matches the picture.

1.

Jamal is in the building.

Jamal is in the balloon.

2.

Katya is on the burglar.

Katya is on the bridge.

3.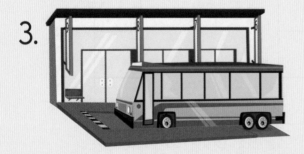

The bus is at the station.

The bus is at the school.

4.

Dad goes to the market.

Dad goes to the mailman.

Word Pictures

COLOR the spaces that show words for **places**.

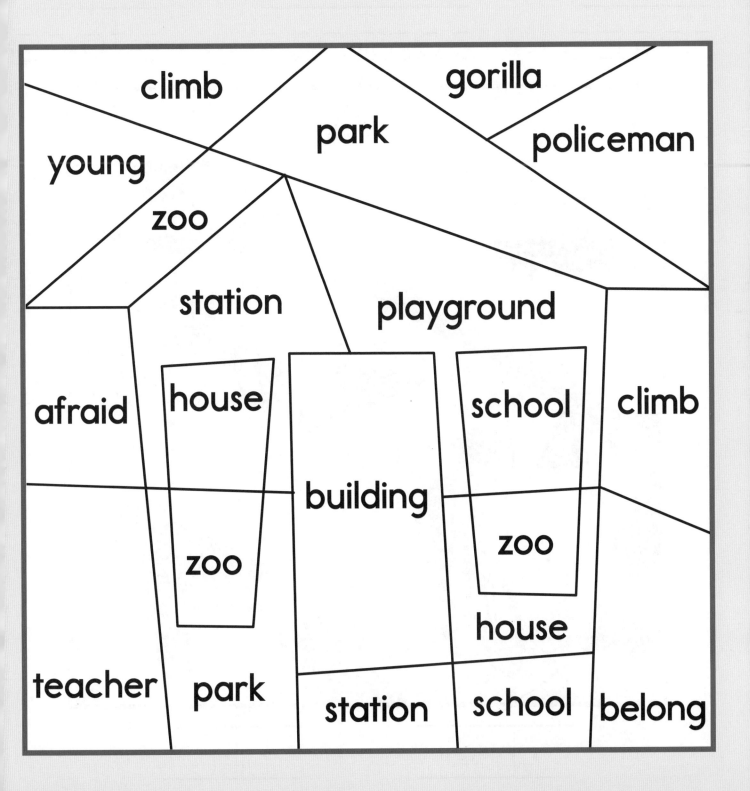

Read and Trace

READ the words and TRACE them. Do you know what they mean?

boat   airplane   taxi

wheel   bike

Match the Meaning

DRAW a line to match the word with its picture.

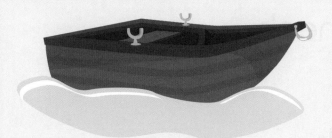

airplane

taxi

boat

bike

Draw It

Help finish the pictures! DRAW or COLOR the things that go to match the sentences.

The airplane has two wheels.

The taxi is yellow.

The bike has blue wheels.

The boat has green spots on it.

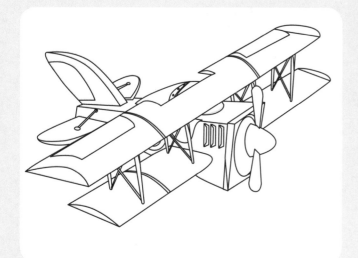

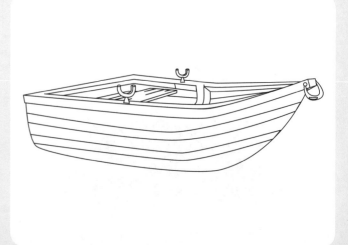

Cross Out

CROSS OUT things that **don't** have **wheels**.

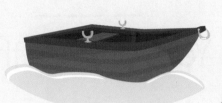

People Actions

Read and Trace

READ the words and TRACE them. Do you know what they mean?

 You bite the hot dog.

 You chase the puppy.

 You listen to your mother.

 You dance to the music.

 You speak to your father.

Blank Out

FINISH each sentence with a word from the word box. CROSS OUT the words as you use them.

> bite   chase   listen   dance   speak

1. You have to _____ if you want to hear.

2. I have a doll that can _____ . She says "Mama!"

3. My dog will _____ any cat he sees.

4. Mom likes to _____ on her toes.

5. I don't like it when bugs _____ me.

Circle It

CIRCLE the words that are **actions**.

1. family   wear   clothes   visit

2. balloon swing   escape pigeon

3. bite   truck   chase   airplane

4. doctor   listen   yours   dance

Right or Wrong?

UNDERLINE the sentence that matches the picture.

1.

The dog climbs the bone.

The dog bites the bone.

2.

I speak on the phone.

I swing on the phone.

3.

Rudy chases the ball.

Rudy climbs the ball.

4.

Bella dances on the rug.

Bella drinks on the rug.

Where Is It?

Read and Trace

READ the words and TRACE them. Do you know what they mean? Where is Doggo?

 between the buildings

 across the street

 beside the stove

 below the bridge

 inside the cage

Draw It

Help finish the picture! COLOR the picture to match the sentences.

The blue balloon is beside the green balloon.

The red balloon is between the yellow balloons.

The orange balloon is below the yellow balloon.

There is a star inside the orange balloon.

Night and Day

DRAW a line to match each word under the moon to its opposite under the sun.

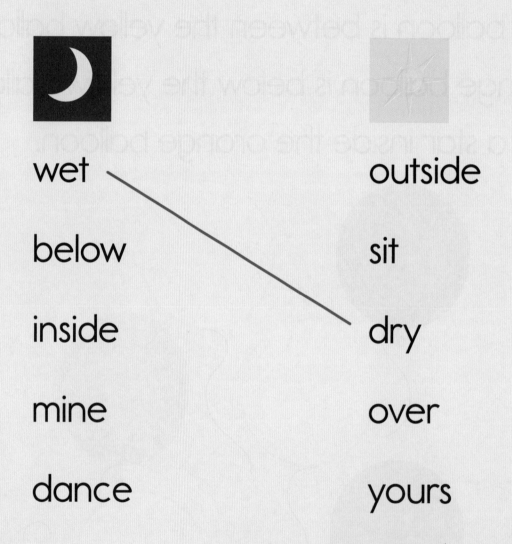

wet   outside

below   sit

inside   dry

mine   over

dance   yours

Find the Friend

READ the clues. Then WRITE the friend's name under each house.

Sasha lives beside Nanci.

Aja lives across the street from Waldo.

Maria lives inside the red house.

Fred lives between Aja and Maria.

Picture Pointers

WRITE the word for each picture clue in the grid.

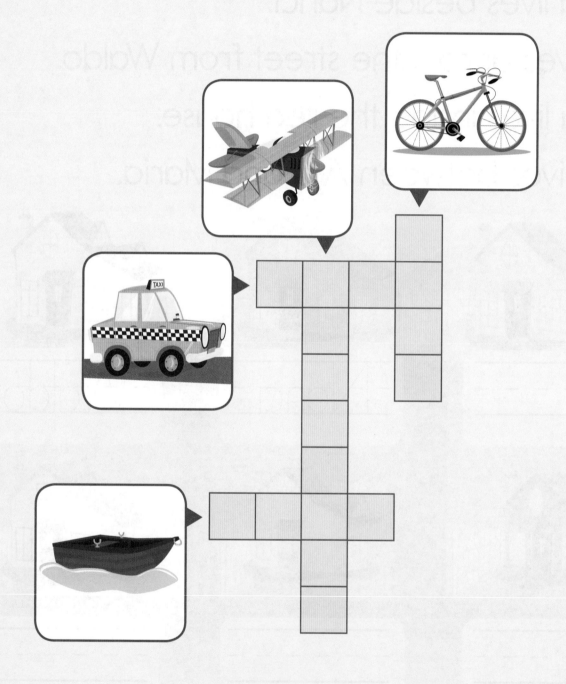

Maze Crazy!

DRAW a line through the words for **people** to get to the crowd. Start at the green arrow.

Start

mother

policeman

bike

wheel

mailman

car

boat

daughter

taxi

airplane

stove

kitchen

doctor

fork

knife

teacher

spoon

End

Draw It

Help finish the picture! DRAW or COLOR the things to match the sentences.

The building across from the market is blue.

The market has a red door.

A dog sits between the bridge and the market.

There is water below the bridge.

Match the Meaning

CIRCLE the picture that matches the word.

colorful

unhappy

his

hide

Review

Right or Wrong?

UNDERLINE the sentence that matches the picture.

1.

   Greg climbs the puppy.

   Greg chases the puppy.

2.

   Gia bikes the hot dog.

   Gia bites the hot dog.

3.

   Tina listens to Mom.

   Tina speaks to Mom.

4.

   Ben likes to dance.

   Ben likes to hide.

Hide and Seek

CIRCLE the things with **wheels** in the picture.

Read and Trace

READ the words and TRACE them. Do you know what they mean?

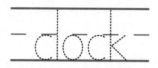

clock

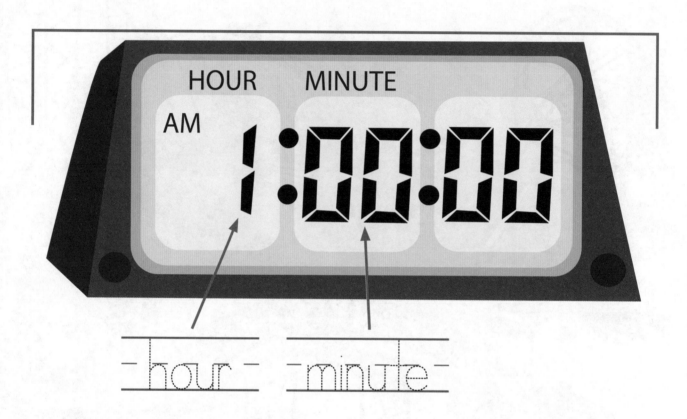

HOUR   MINUTE

AM

hour   minute

1 day = 24 hours

1 hour = 60 minutes

What time is it on your clock? _____

calendar

year

	JANUARY							FEBRUARY							MARCH							APRIL							MAY							JUNE					
S	M	T	W	T	F	S	S	M	T	W	T	F	S	S	M	T	W	T	F	S	S	M	T	W	T	F	S	S	M	T	W	T	F	S	S	M	T	W	T	F	S
					1	2	3		1	2	3	4	5	6	7		1	2	3	4	5	6	7				1	2	3	4					1	2		1	2	3	4	5	6

(calendar grid for all twelve months)

JANUARY
S M T W T F S
            1 2 3
4 5 6 7 8 9 10
11 12 13 14 15 16 17
18 19 20 21 22 23 24
25 26 27 28 29 30 31

FEBRUARY
S M T W T F S
1 2 3 4 5 6 7
8 9 10 11 12 13 14
15 16 17 18 19 20 21
22 23 24 25 26 27 28

MARCH
S M T W T F S
1 2 3 4 5 6 7
8 9 10 11 12 13 14
15 16 17 18 19 20 21
22 23 24 25 26 27 28
29 30 31

APRIL
S M T W T F S
         1 2 3 4
5 6 7 8 9 10 11
12 13 14 15 16 17 18
19 20 21 22 23 24 25
26 27 28 29 30

MAY
S M T W T F S
               1 2
3 4 5 6 7 8 9
10 11 12 13 14 15 16
17 18 19 20 21 22 23
24 25 26 27 28 29 30
31

JUNE
S M T W T F S
   1 2 3 4 5 6
7 8 9 10 11 12 13
14 15 16 17 18 19 20
21 22 23 24 25 26 27
28 29 30

JULY
S M T W T F S
      1 2 3 4
5 6 7 8 9 10 11
12 13 14 15 16 17 18
19 20 21 22 23 24 25
26 27 28 29 30 31

AUGUST
S M T W T F S
                  1
2 3 4 5 6 7 8
9 10 11 12 13 14 15
16 17 18 19 20 21 22
23 24 25 26 27 28 29
30 31

SEPTEMBER
S M T W T F S
      1 2 3 4 5
6 7 8 9 10 11 12
13 14 15 16 17 18 19
20 21 22 23 24 25 26
27 28 29 30

OCTOBER
S M T W T F S
            1 2 3
4 5 6 7 8 9 10
11 12 13 14 15 16 17
18 19 20 21 22 23 24
25 26 27 28 29 30 31

NOVEMBER
S M T W T F S
1 2 3 4 5 6 7
8 9 10 11 12 13 14
15 16 17 18 19 20 21
22 23 24 25 26 27 28
29 30

DECEMBER
S M T W T F S
         1 2 3 4 5
6 7 8 9 10 11 12
13 14 15 16 17 18 19
20 21 22 23 24 25 26
27 28 29 30 31

month

date

7 days = 1 week

12 months = 1 year

What is today's date?

_____

_____

It's Time for Time

Blank Out!

FINISH each sentence with a word from the word box. CROSS OUT the words as you use them.

year	month	clock	calendar	hour

1. Use the _____ to see the time.

2. There are 60 minutes in an _____.

3. Lia's birthday is in the _____ of April.

4. The _____ shows the days of the week.

5. There are 12 months in a _____.

Right or Wrong?

UNDERLINE the sentence that matches the picture.

1.

It will be 9:52 in one hour.

It will be 9:52 in one month.

2.

It will be 9:52 in one month.

Next month it will be 2012.

Next year it will be 2012.

3.

May 15 is the date of the party.

May 15 is the month of the party.

4.

It will be 10:05 in five minutes.

It will be 10:05 in five hours.

Days of the Week

Read and Trace

READ the words and TRACE them.
Do you know what they mean?

JULY						
S	**M**	**T**	**W**	**T**	**F**	**S**
			1	2	3	4
5	6	7	8	9	10	11
12	13	14	15	16	17	18
19	20	21	22	23	24	25
26	27	28	29	30	31	

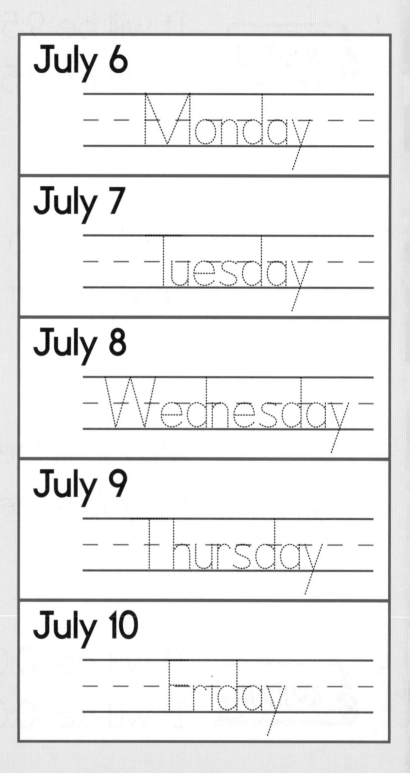

July 6

Monday

July 7

Tuesday

July 8

Wednesday

July 9

Thursday

July 10

Friday

July 11
Saturday

July 12
Sunday

Weekdays = Monday, Tuesday, Wednesday, Thursday, Friday

Weekend = Saturday and Sunday

What day is today? _____

Days of the Week

Blank Out

FILL IN the blanks with the missing days of the week. CROSS OUT the words as you use them.

Friday   Monday   Sunday   Tuesday   Wednesday

Monday, _____ , Wednesday
1

Thursday, _____ , Saturday
2

Saturday, _____ , Monday
3

Tuesday, _____ , Thursday
4

Sunday, _____ , Tuesday
5

Criss Cross

WRITE the word for each clue in the grid.

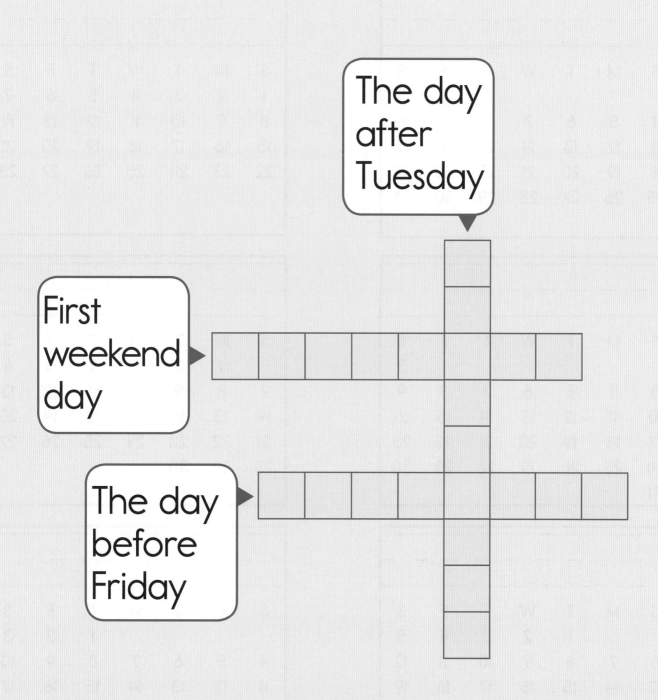

The day after Tuesday

First weekend day

The day before Friday

Months of the Year

Read and Trace

READ the words and TRACE them.

January

S	M	T	W	T	F	S
				1	2	3
4	5	6	7	8	9	10
11	12	13	14	15	16	17
18	19	20	21	22	23	24
25	26	27	28	29	30	31

February

S	M	T	W	T	F	S
1	2	3	4	5	6	7
8	9	10	11	12	13	14
15	16	17	18	19	20	21
22	23	24	25	26	27	28

May

S	M	T	W	T	F	S
					1	2
3	4	5	6	7	8	9
10	11	12	13	14	15	16
17	18	19	20	21	22	23
24	25	26	27	28	29	30
31						

June

S	M	T	W	T	F	S
	1	2	3	4	5	6
7	8	9	10	11	12	13
14	15	16	17	18	19	20
21	22	23	24	25	26	27
28	29	30				

September

S	M	T	W	T	F	S
		1	2	3	4	5
6	7	8	9	10	11	12
13	14	15	16	17	18	19
20	21	22	23	24	25	26
27	28	29	30			

October

S	M	T	W	T	F	S
				1	2	3
4	5	6	7	8	9	10
11	12	13	14	15	16	17
18	19	20	21	22	23	24
25	26	27	28	29	30	31

March

S	M	T	W	T	F	S
1	2	3	4	5	6	7
8	9	10	11	12	13	14
15	16	17	18	19	20	21
22	23	24	25	26	27	28
29	30	31				

April

S	M	T	W	T	F	S
			1	2	3	4
5	6	7	8	9	10	11
12	13	14	15	16	17	18
19	20	21	22	23	24	25
26	27	28	29	30		

July

S	M	T	W	T	F	S
			1	2	3	4
5	6	7	8	9	10	11
12	13	14	15	16	17	18
19	20	21	22	23	24	25
26	27	28	29	30	31	

August

S	M	T	W	T	F	S
						1
2	3	4	5	6	7	8
9	10	11	12	13	14	15
16	17	18	19	20	21	22
23	24	25	26	27	28	29
30	31					

November

S	M	T	W	T	F	S
1	2	3	4	5	6	7
8	9	10	11	12	13	14
15	16	17	18	19	20	21
22	23	24	25	26	27	28
29	30					

December

S	M	T	W	T	F	S
		1	2	3	4	5
6	7	8	9	10	11	12
13	14	15	16	17	18	19
20	21	22	23	24	25	26
27	28	29	30	31		

Criss Cross

WRITE the word for each clue in the grid.

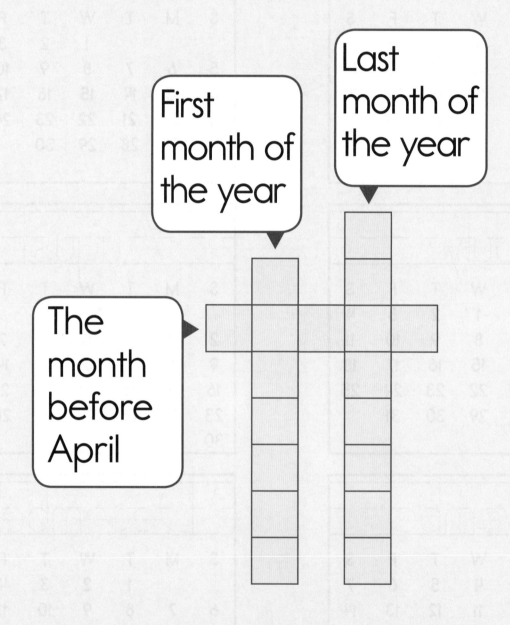

Blank Out

FILL IN the blanks with the missing months of the year. CROSS OUT the words as you use them.

August   February   January   May   November

January, _____ , March
1

April, _____ , June
2

July, _____ , September
3

October, _____ , December
4

December, _____ , February
5

Read and Trace

READ the words and TRACE them. Do you know what they mean?

morning

noon

afternoon   evening   night

Criss Cross

WRITE the word for each clue in the grid.

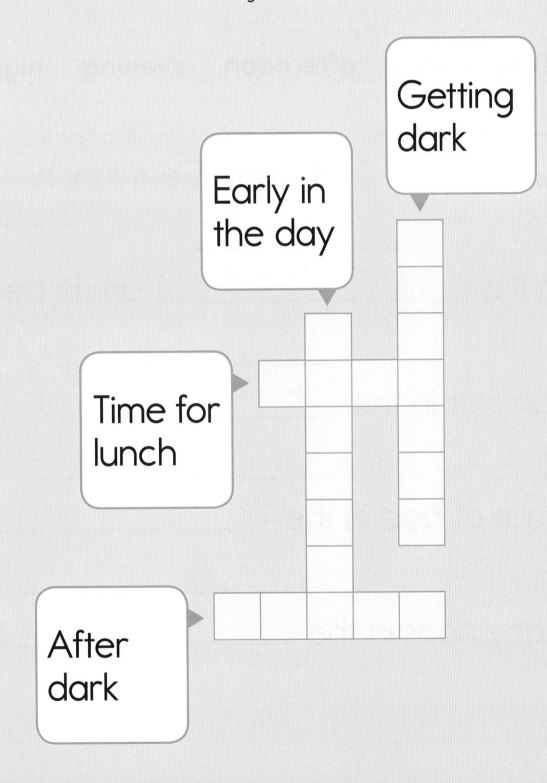

Getting dark

Early in the day

Time for lunch

After dark

Blank Out

FINISH each sentence with a word from the word box. CROSS OUT the words as you use them.

morning   Noon   afternoon   evening   night

_____ is when I eat lunch.
1

When it is _____, I am in bed.
2

The sun sets in the _____.
3

I get out of bed in the _____.
4

The baby naps in the _____.
5

Night and Day

DRAW a line to match each word under the moon to its opposite under the sun.

before   evening

night   after

early   late

light   day

morning   dark

Read and Trace

READ the words and TRACE them. Do you know what they mean?

meal

breakfast

lunch

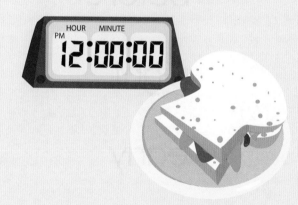

snack

dinner

Match the Meaning

DRAW a line to match the meal with its time.

breakfast

lunch

snack

dinner

Let's Eat!

Blank Out!

FINISH each sentence with a word from the box. CROSS OUT the words as you use them.

breakfast   lunch   dinner   snack   meal

1. I wash my hands before every _____.

2. We eat _____ in the morning.

3. Noon is time for _____.

4. I eat a _____ between lunch and dinner.

5. We eat _____ in the evening.

Right or Wrong?

UNDERLINE the sentence that matches the picture.

1.

It is time for dinner.

It is time for lunch.

2.

What a yummy snack!

What a yummy dinner!

3.

It is time for dinner.

It is time for breakfast.

4.

That's a big mail.

That's a big meal.

Actions All Day Long

Read and Trace

READ the words and TRACE them.
Do you know what they mean?

To _wake_ is to stop sleeping and get out of bed.

To _start_ is to begin something.

To _finish_ is to end something .

To _hurry_ is to go fast. If you are late, you have to rush.

To _leave_ is to go out. Goodbye!

Match the Meaning

DRAW a line to match the words that have the **same** meaning..

start   get up

finish   begin

hurry   end

leave   go fast

wake   go

Find the Friend

READ the clues. Then WRITE the friend's name under each picture.

Guy leaves the pool.

Yasmin finishes her dinner.

Ben starts a picture.

Tony wakes up.

_____

- - - - - - - - - - -

_____

_____

- - - - - - - - - - -

_____

_____

- - - - - - - - - - -

_____

_____

- - - - - - - - - - -

_____

Word Pictures

COLOR the spaces that show words for **actions**.

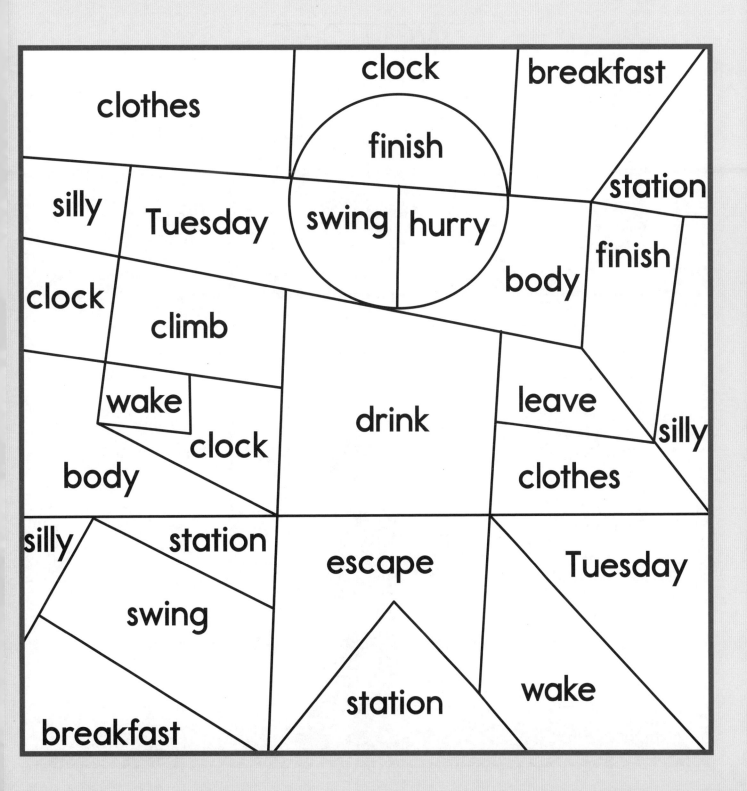

clock

clothes

breakfast

finish

silly

Tuesday

swing | hurry

station

finish

body

clock

climb

wake

clock

drink

leave

silly

body

clothes

silly

station

escape

Tuesday

swing

station

wake

breakfast

What's the Weather?

Read and Trace

READ the words and TRACE them. Do you know what they mean?

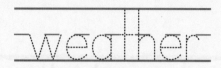

weather

rainy

sunny

cloudy

foggy

windy

Picture Pointers

WRITE the word for each picture clue in the grid.

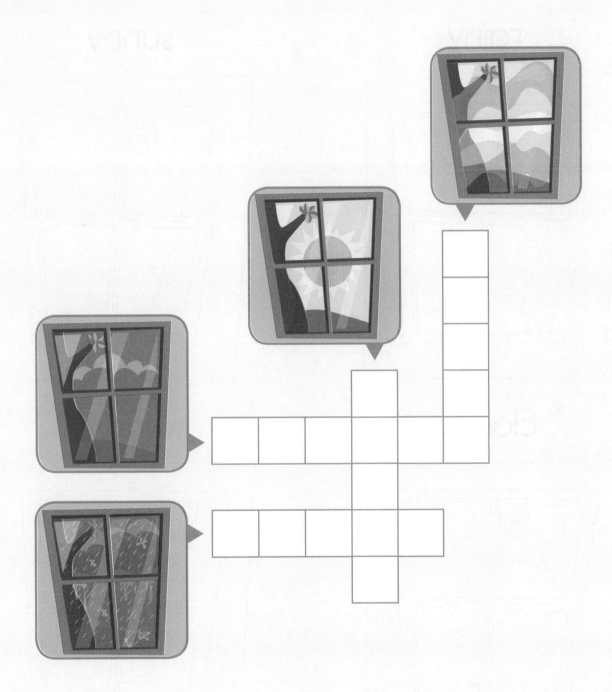

What's the Weather?

Draw It!

Help finish the pictures! Draw the pictures to match the words. Then COLOR the pictures.

rainy

sunny

cloudy

windy

Blank Out

FINISH each sentence with a word from the word box. CROSS OUT the words as you use them.

foggy   sunny   rainy   windy   weather

1. We will eat outside if the _____ is good.

2. It is hard to see far on a _____ day.

3. Your feet will get wet on a _____ day.

4. I hope it is hot and _____ on my birthday.

5. It was so _____, Marla's hat blew off!

Circle It

CIRCLE the words that are about **time**.

1. hour   nose   date   shirt

2. thirsty   year   float   day

3. belong   clock   minute   chase

4. calendar   bite   yours   month

Maze Crazy!

DRAW a line through the words for **weather** to get to the things for a rainy winter day. Start at the green arrow.

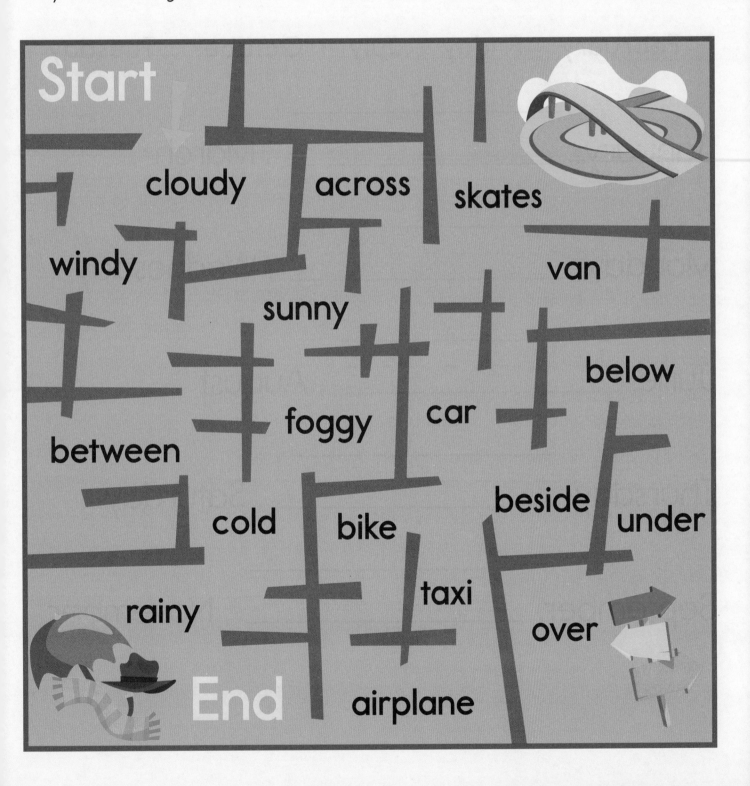

Start

cloudy   across   skates

windy   van

sunny

below

foggy   car

between

beside   under

cold   bike

taxi

rainy   over

End   airplane

237

Blank Out

FILL IN the blanks with the missing months or days from the box. CROSS OUT the words as you use them.

February   Friday   July   October   Tuesday

January, _____ 1 , March

Monday, _____ 2 , Wednesday

June, _____ 3 , August

Thursday, _____ 4 , Saturday

September, _____ 5 , November

Criss Cross

WRITE the word for each clue in the grid.

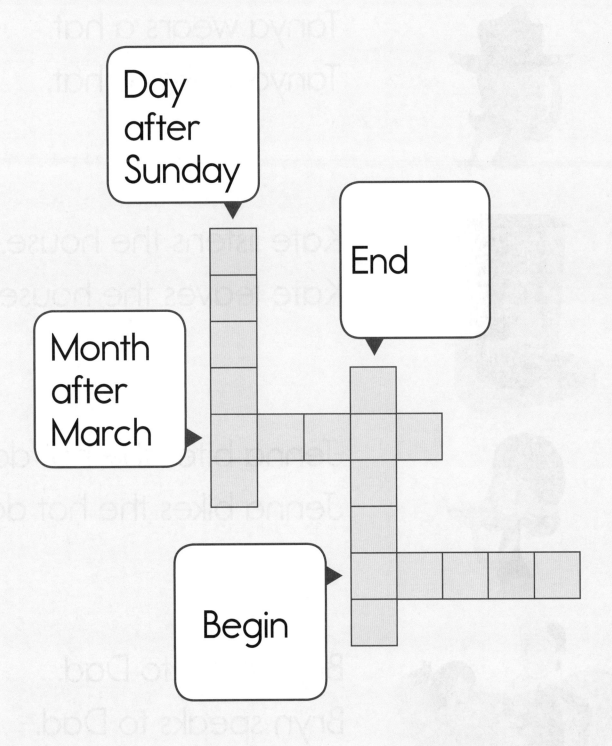

Day after Sunday

End

Month after March

Begin

Right or Wrong?

UNDERLINE the sentence that matches the picture.

1.

   Tanya wears a hat.

   Tanya wakes a hat.

2.

   Kate listens the house.

   Kate leaves the house.

3.

   Jenna bites the hot dog.

   Jenna bikes the hot dog.

4.

   Bryn starts to Dad.

   Bryn speaks to Dad.

Index

across: on the other side of

action: something you do

afraid: scared

afternoon: the time between noon and evening

airplane:

angry: mad

April: the 4th month of the year

August: the 8th month of the year

balloon:

belong: when you have or own something, it's yours

below: under

beside: next to

between: in the middle

bike:

bite: chomp with your teeth

boat:

body:

bone:

breakfast: the first meal of the day

bridge:

building:

burglar:

button:

cage:

calendar:

chase: to run after something or someone

climb: to go up, like on a ladder or in a tree

clock:

clothes:

cloudy:

coat:

colorful: having lots of colors, like a rainbow

cook: to make food hot on a stove or in an oven

dance: to move your body to music

date: the day of the year, like May 5, 2010

daughter: the girl child of a mother or father

December: the last month of the year

dinner: the last meal of the day

doctor:

drink: to swallow something liquid like milk or water

dry: the opposite of wet

escape: to run away or get out of a cage

evening: the time of day when it starts to get dark

family:

father: a man who has a child

February: the 2nd month of the year

finger:

finish: to end

float: to bob on top of the water

foggy:

fork:

Friday: the day of the week after Thursday

gorilla:

hers: belonging to her

hide: to go where no one can see you

his: belonging to him

hour: 60 minutes

hungry: needing to eat something

hurry: to rush, or go fast

inside: the opposite of outside

January: the 1st month of the year

jeans:

July: the 7th month of the year

June: the 6th month of the year

kangaroo:

kitchen:

knife:

leave: to go out

leopard:

listen: to hear

lunch: the meal you eat in the middle of the day

241

Index

mailman:

March: the 3rd month of the year

market:

May: the 5th month of the year

meal: food that you eat at a set time of day

mine: belonging to me

minute: part of an hour. There are 60 minutes in an hour.

Monday: the day of the week after Sunday

month: part of a year, like April. There are 12 months in a year.

morning: early in the day

mother: a woman who has a child

my: belonging to me

night: after dark

noon: 12 p.m.

nose:

November: the 11th month of the year

October: the 10th month of the year

ours: belonging to us

penguin:

pigeon:

playground:

policeman:

pool:

rainy:

Saturday: the day of the week after Friday

September: the 9th month of the year

sharp: pointy, something that can cut

shirt:

silly: funny, acting odd or crazy

skates:

snack: food you eat between meals

son: the boy child of a mother or father

speak: to say something

spoon:

start: to begin

station:

stove:

Sunday: the day of the week after Saturday

sunny:

swing: to move back and forth, like on a rope

taxi:

teacher: a person who shows others a lesson

teeth:

thirsty: dry, wanting to drink something

Thursday: the day of the week after Wednesday

Tuesday: the day of the week after Monday

unhappy: sad

visit: to go see a person or a place

wake: to stop sleeping and get up

walrus:

wash: to clean with soap and water

wear: to put clothes on your body

weather: what it's like outside—rainy, sunny, or cold

Wednesday: the day of the week after Tuesday

wheels:

windy:

year: 12 months, or 365 days

young: the opposite of old

yours: belonging to you

Answers

Page 127

b
o
n
f i n g e r
o
s
e

Page 128

Page 129

Page 131

mother
father
son
daughter

Page 132
1. Mother hugs the baby.
2. Father and son eat.
3. This is a family.
4. The daughter is happy.

Page 133

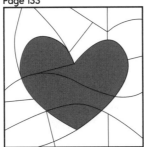

Page 135
1. stove
2. knife
3. spoon
4. kitchen
5. fork

Page 136
Suggestions:

Page 137

Page 139

c
c o a t
l
o
t
h   b
e   u
s h i r t
t   o
n

Page 140

Chuck   Tim

Ken   Pam

Page 141

Page 143

wear
wash
cook
drink
visit

Page 144
1. eat, run
2. play, wash
3. wear, hug
4. visit, cook

Page 145
1. I wash my hands.
2. I visit my granny.
3. I wear my mittens.
4. Bob drinks juice.

Page 147

unhappy   angry

afraid   happy

Page 148
1. sad, angry
2. afraid, happy
3. thirsty
4. hungry, mad

Page 149
afraid → scared
unhappy → sad
angry → mad
drink → sip
sleep → nap

Page 150

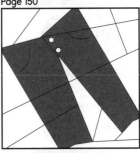

Page 151

k n i f e
a   s
t h i r s t y
l   o
y   v
e

Page 152
1. arm, eyes
2. leg, finger
3. nose, teeth
4. face, lips

Page 153
1. Father is angry.
2. Jill wears a hat.
3. Sam cut his finger.
4. Mother cooks eggs.

Page 154

Answers

Page 155
1. NO
2. YES
3. NO
4. NO
5. YES

Page 157

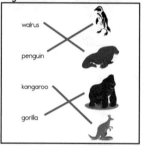

Page 158

Page 159

Page 161
1. YES
2. NO
3. NO
4. NO
5. YES

Page 162

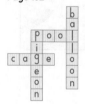

Page 163

Page 165
1. The balloon floats in the air.
2. I climb the tree.
3. The baby kangaroo is hiding.
4. The pigeon escapes.

Page 166
1. hide, see
2. drink, wear
3. swings, floats
4. escape, climb

Page 167

Page 169

Page 170
1. silly
2. sharp
3. colorful
4. dry
5. young

Page 171
wet → dry
unhappy → happy
hot → cold
young → old
gray → colorful

Page 174
1. mine
2. his
3. yours
4. her
5. ours

Page 175
Lori → Lori's
me → mine
you → yours
him → his
her → hers
us → ours

Page 176
1. monkey, rat
2. walrus, penguin
3. pigeon, kangaroo
4. gorilla, leopard

Page 177
1. NO
2. NO
3. YES
4. NO
5. NO

Page 178

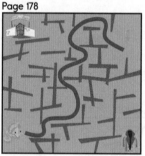

Page 179
1. kitchen
2. float
3. escaped
4. belongs
5. afraid

Page 180
1. The dog has a bone.
2. The kid climbs a tree.
3. The penguin is in a cage.
4. Jan swings in the yard.

Page 181

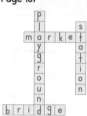

Page 183

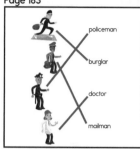

Page 184
1. people
2. doctor
3. mailman
4. teacher
5. policeman

Page 185

Page 187

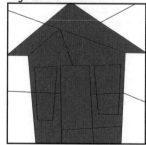

Page 188
1. Jamal is in the building.
2. Katya is on the bridge.
3. The bus is at the station.
4. Dad goes to the market.

Page 189

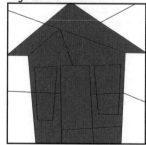

244

Answers

Page 191

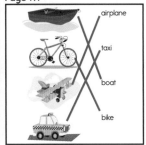

airplane
taxi
boat
bike

Page 192

Page 193

Page 195
1. listen
2. speak
3. chase
4. dance
5. bite

Page 196
1. wear, visit
2. swing, escape
3. bite, chase
4. listen, dance

Page 197
1. The dog bites the bone.
2. I speak on the phone.
3. Rudy chases the ball.
4. Bella dances on the rug.

Page 199

Page 200
wet → dry
below → over
inside → outside
mine → yours
dance → sit

Page 201

Sasha   Nanci   Waldo
Maria   Fred   Aja

Page 202

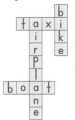

t a x i
  i   b
a i r   i
p   k
l   e
b o a t
  n
  e

Page 203

Page 204

Page 205

Page 206
1. Greg chases the puppy.
2. Gia bites the hot dog.
3. Tina listens to Mom.
4. Ben likes to dance.

Page 207

Page 210
1. clock
2. hour
3. month
4. calendar
5. year

Page 211
1. It will be 9:52 in one hour.
2. Next year it will be 2012.
3. May 15 is the date of the party.
4. It will be 10:05 in five minutes.

Page 214
1. Tuesday
2. Friday
3. Sunday
4. Wednesday
5. Monday

Page 215

W
S a t u r d a y
  e
T h u r s d a y
  n
  e
  s
  d
  a
  y

Page 218

D
M a r c h
J   e
a   c
n   e
u   m
a   b
r   e
y   r

Page 219
1. February
2. May
3. August
4. November
5. January

Page 221

e
v
m e n i n g
n o o n
r   i
n   n
i   g
n
night

Page 222
1. Noon
2. night
3. evening
4. morning
5. afternoon

Page 223
before → after
night → day
early → late
light → dark
morning → evening

Answers

Page 225

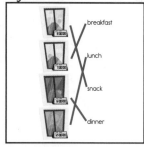

breakfast
lunch
snack
dinner

Page 226
1. meal
2. breakfast
3. lunch
4. snack
5. dinner

Page 227
1. It is time for lunch.
2. What a yummy snack!
3. It is time for dinner.
4. That's a big meal.

Page 229
start → begin
finish → end
hurry → go fast
leave → go
wake → get up

Page 230

Tony
Ben
Yasmin
Guy

Page 231

Page 233

f
o
g
g
s y
c l o u d y
u
r a i n n
y

Page 234

Page 235
1. weather
2. foggy
3. rainy
4. sunny
5. windy

Page 236
1. hour, date
2. year, day
3. clock, minute
4. calendar, month

Page 237

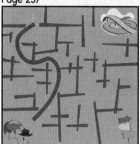

Page 238
1. February
2. Tuesday
3. July
4. Friday
5. October

Page 239

M
o
n
d f
A p r i l
y n
i
s t a r t
h

Page 240
1. Tanya wears a hat.
2. Kate leaves the house.
3. Jenna bites the hot dog.
4. Bryn speaks to Dad.

1st Grade
Math
Games & Puzzles

Contents

Connect the Dots

DRAW a line to connect the numbers in order, starting with I.

Safe Crackers

WRITE the sums. Then WRITE the sums from smallest to largest to find the right combination for the safe.

5	3	1	1	6	8
+ 2	+ 3	+ 4	+ 1	+ 3	+ 0
7					
1	2	3	4	5	6

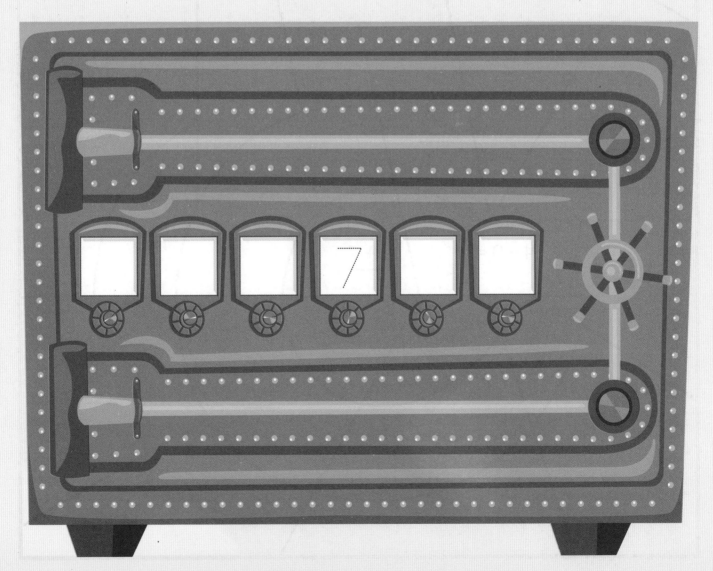

Mystery Number

WRITE the sums, and COLOR each section according to the numbers to reveal the mystery number.

8 =   10 =   5 =   4 =   7 =

$$7 + 1$$

$$5 + 2 =$$

$$1 + 3 =$$

$$9 + 1$$

$$5 + 0$$

$$4 + 1$$

$$4 + 6$$

$$2 + 2$$

$$2 + 6$$

$$1 + 6$$

$$4 + 3$$

$$2 + 3$$

$$4 + 4$$

$$3 + 2$$

$$8 + 2$$

$$4 + 0 =$$

$$0 + 7$$

$$4 + 0$$

$$7 + 3$$

$$2 + 2$$

$$10 + 0$$

$$0 + 5$$

$$3 + 5$$

$$1 + 4 =$$

$$1 + 3 =$$

Code Breaker

SOLVE each problem. Then WRITE the letter or number that matches each sum to solve the riddle.

| 3
+ 1
4
₁
U | 8
+ 2
₂
B | 5
+ 4
₃
A | 2
+ 4
₄
7 | 3
+ 5
₅
S | 1
+ 0
₆
8 |

| 4
+ 1
₇
E | 5
+ 2
₈
9 | 2
+ 1
₉
C |

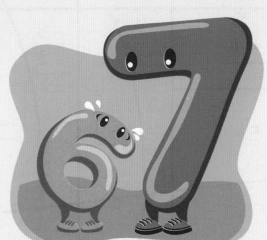

Why is 6 afraid of 7?

___ ___ ___ U̇ ___ ___ ___
10   5   3   9   4   8   5

___ ___ ___!
6   1   7

Subtracting Differences from 10

Mystery Number

WRITE the differences, and COLOR each section according to the differences to reveal the mystery number.

1 =   2 =   3 =   4 =   5 =

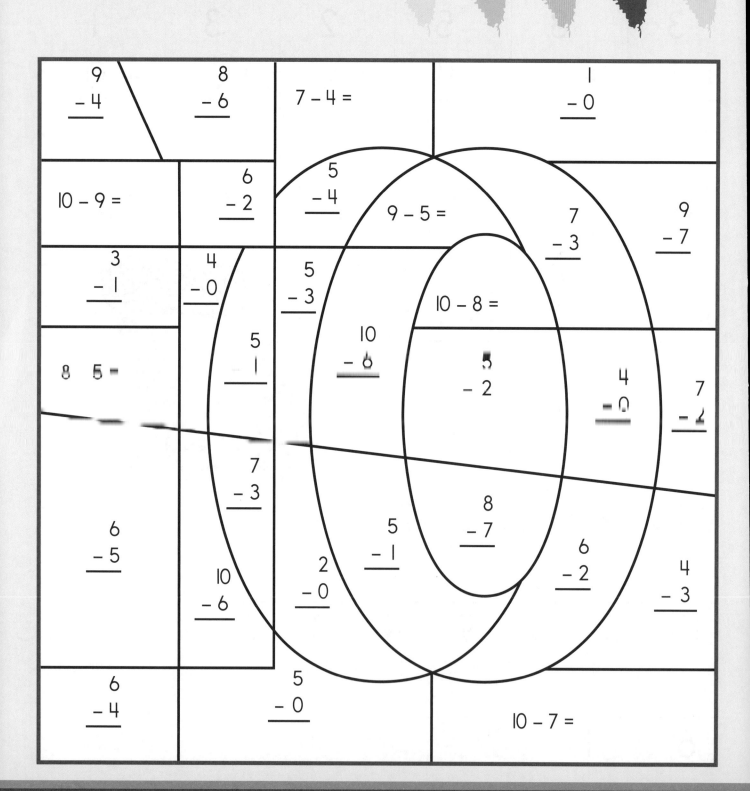

Space Walk

Using the numbers in the picture, WRITE as many fact families with the number 9 as you can.

HINT: A fact family shows all of the different ways that three numbers can be added and subtracted.

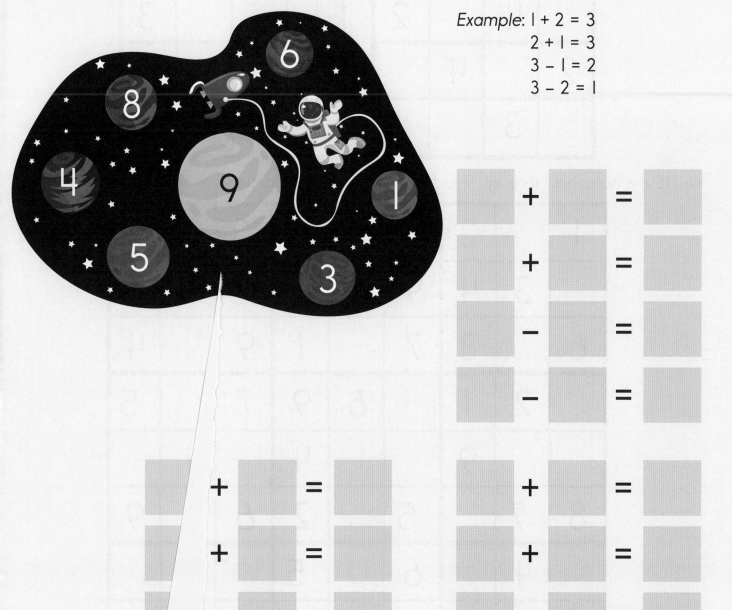

Example: 1 + 2 = 3
2 + 1 = 3
3 − 1 = 2
3 − 2 = 1

Super Sudoku

WRITE the numbers 1 through 4 so that each row, column, and box has all four numbers.

WRITE the numbers 1 through 9 so that each row, column, and box has all nine numbers.

Pipe Down

WRITE the missing number. Then FOLLOW the pipe, and WRITE the same number in the next problem.

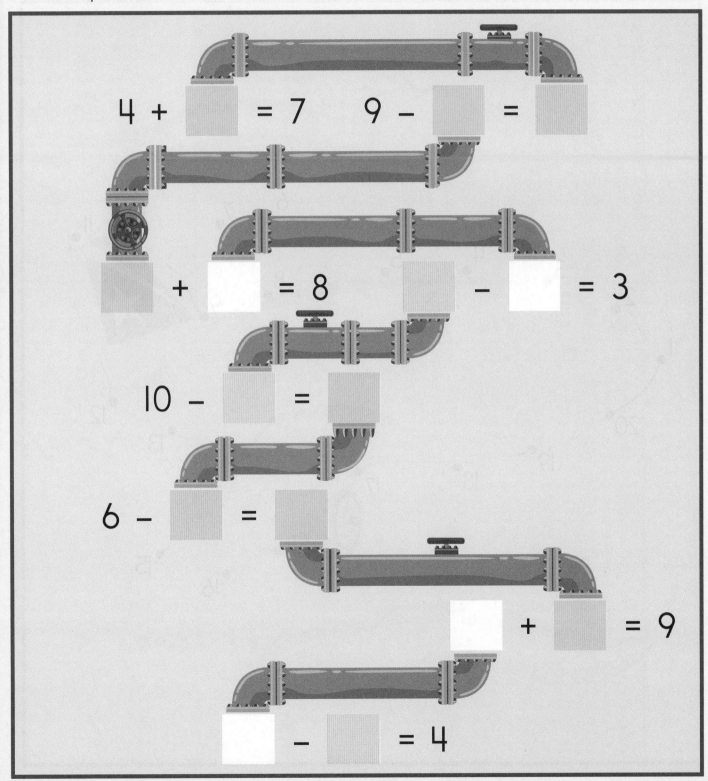

4 + ☐ = 7   9 – ☐ = ☐

☐ + ☐ = 8   ☐ – ☐ = 3

10 – ☐ = ☐

6 – ☐ = ☐

☐ + ☐ = 9

☐ – ☐ = 4

Connect the Dots

DRAW a line to connect the numbers in order, starting with 1.

Ant Farm

The signs are in the wrong places. DRAW a line from each sign to the ant farm where it belongs.

15 Ants

16 Ants

18 Ants

14 Ants

Safe Crackers

WRITE the sums. Then WRITE the sums from smallest to largest to find the right combination for the safe.

$$\begin{array}{r} 7 \\ + 8 \\ \hline \end{array}$$

$$\begin{array}{r} 10 \\ + 10 \\ \hline \end{array}$$

$$\begin{array}{r} 3 \\ + 9 \\ \hline \end{array}$$

$$\begin{array}{r} 6 \\ + 5 \\ \hline \end{array}$$

$$\begin{array}{r} 9 \\ + 9 \\ \hline \end{array}$$

$$\begin{array}{r} 8 \\ + 6 \\ \hline \end{array}$$

1 2 3 4 5 6

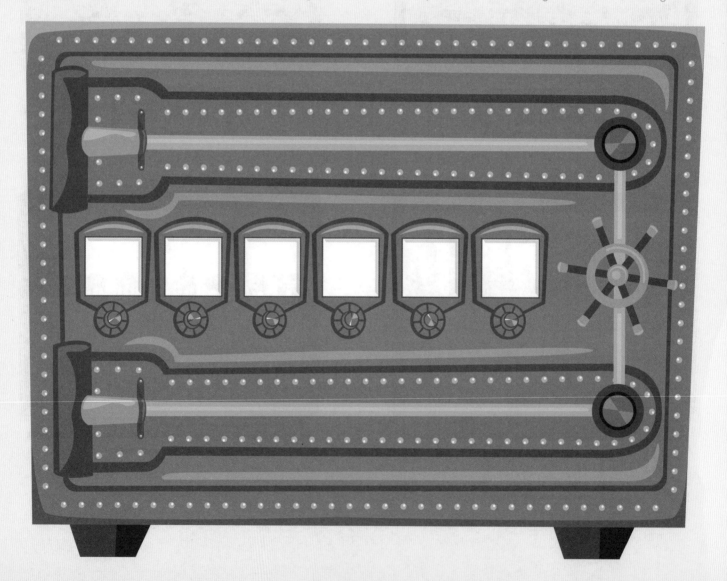

Spin It

Use the spinner from page 362. SPIN the spinner once for each problem, and WRITE the number in the blue box. Then WRITE the sum in the red box. (Save the spinner to use again.)

9 + ☐ = ☐

☐ + 7 = ☐

☐ + 10 = ☐

6 + ☐ = ☐

8 + ☐ = ☐

☐ + 9 = ☐

☐ + 7 = ☐

10 + ☐ = ☐

6 + ☐ = ☐

☐ + 8 = ☐

Your Deal

Using the number cards 2 through 10 from a deck of playing cards, DEAL a card onto each space. SAY the sum out loud. REPEAT until you have run out of cards.

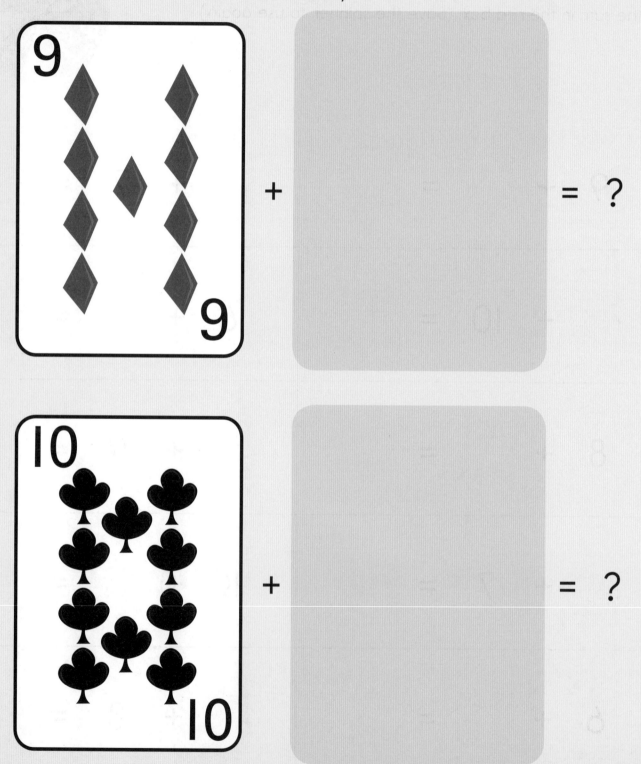

Space Walk

Using the numbers in the picture, WRITE as many fact families with the number 17 as you can.

☐ + ☐ = ☐

☐ + ☐ = ☐

☐ − ☐ = ☐

☐ − ☐ = ☐

☐ + ☐ = ☐   ☐ + ☐ = ☐

☐ + ☐ = ☐   ☐ + ☐ = ☐

☐ − ☐ = ☐   ☐ − ☐ = ☐

☐ − ☐ = ☐   ☐ − ☐ = ☐

Magic Square

WRITE the numbers 1 through 9 in the square so that every group of three numbers across, down, and diagonally has a sum of 15.

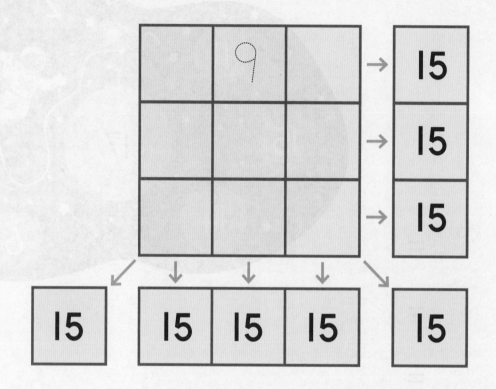

Crossing Paths

WRITE the missing numbers.

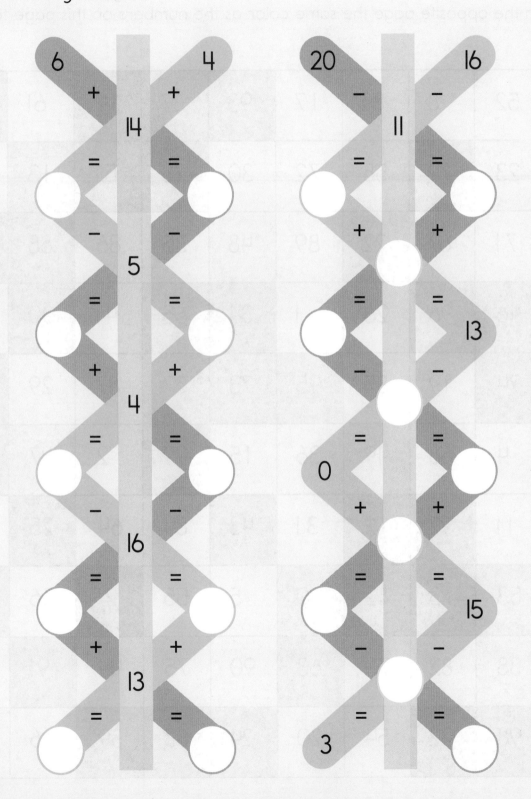

Color Mix-up

These squares are all the right colors, but they're in the wrong order. COLOR the squares on the opposite page the same color as the numbers on this page to see the design.

45	52	8	81	17	93	37	14	61	28
18	23	79	58	72	30	78	51	13	80
60	71	67	22	89	48	35	86	68	94
9	46	96	26	1	34	65	41	100	16
88	74	19	85	95	73	57	87	29	77
27	4	66	49	36	15	99	2	47	59
33	11	92	12	31	43	84	64	25	7
76	53	3	62	50	5	55	21	56	97
42	38	82	70	63	90	75	44	91	40
10	98	32	54	20	24	83	39	6	69

7

1	2	3	4	5	6	7	8	9	10
11	12	13	14	15	16	17	18	19	20
21	22	23	24	25	26	27	28	29	30
31	32	33	34	35	36	37	38	39	40
41	42	43	44	45	46	47	48	49	50
51	52	53	54	55	56	57	58	59	60
61	62	63	64	65	66	67	68	69	70
71	72	73	74	75	76	77	78	79	80
81	82	83	84	85	86	87	88	89	90
91	92	93	94	95	96	97	98	99	100

Super Spies

WRITE the missing numbers in the chart. DECODE the note on the opposite page, using the letters in those squares.

1	O 2	3	4	5	6	7	8	C	10
11	12	L	T	15	16	17	N	19	20
21	22	23	24	25	26	27	28	29	30
31	32	33	34	35	P	37	38	39	E
41	S	43	44	45	46	47	48	49	50
51	52	53	V	55	56	57	58	I	60
K	62	63	64	65	66	H	68	69	70
71	72	73	74	75	76	77	78	79	80
81	82	83	84	A	86	87	88	89	90
R	92	93	94	95	96	97	98	99	D

——   ——   ——   ——   ——   ——   ——   ——   ——
14   67   40   42   40   9   91   40   14

——   ——   ——   ——   ——   ——   ——   ——
36   13   85   18   42   85   91   40

——   ——   ——   ——   ——   ——   ——   ——
67   59   100   100   40   18   59   18

——   ——   ——   ——   ——   ——   ——
14   67   40   54   85   42   40

◯   ——   ——   ——   ——
2   18   14   67   40

——   ——   ——   —— .
100   40   42   61

Hidden Design

COUNT the tens and ones. Then COLOR the squares that match the numbers to see the hidden design.

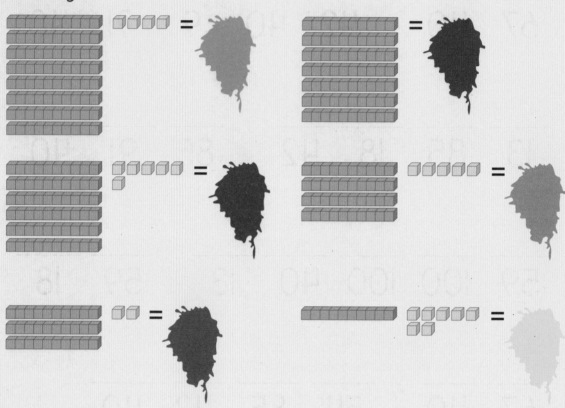

66	66	66	66	66	66	66	66
66	84	84	84	84	84	84	84
84	84	17	17	17	17	17	17
17	17	17	45	45	45	45	45
45	45	45	45	32	32	32	32
32	32	32	32	32	70	70	70
70	70	70	70	70	70	66	66
66	66	66	66	66	66	66	84

Safe Crackers

WRITE the number for each picture. Then WRITE the digit in the tens place of each number from largest to smallest to find the combination for the safe.

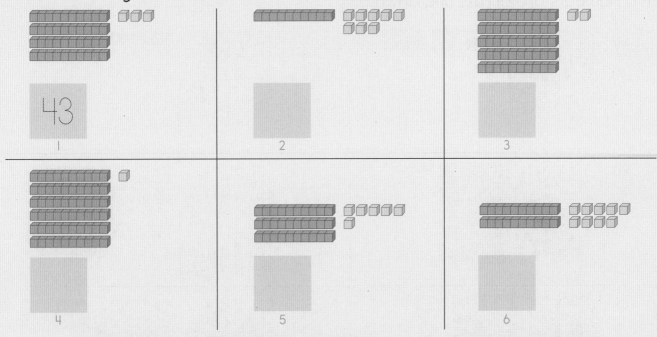

1. 43
2.
3.

4.
5.
6.

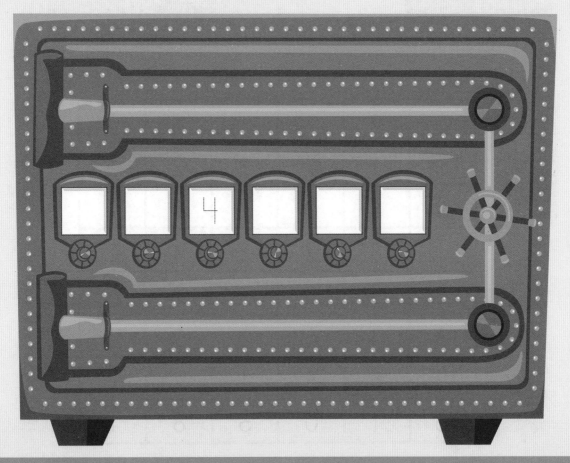

Number Search

WRITE the number for each picture. Then CIRCLE it in the puzzle.

HINT: Numbers are across and down only.

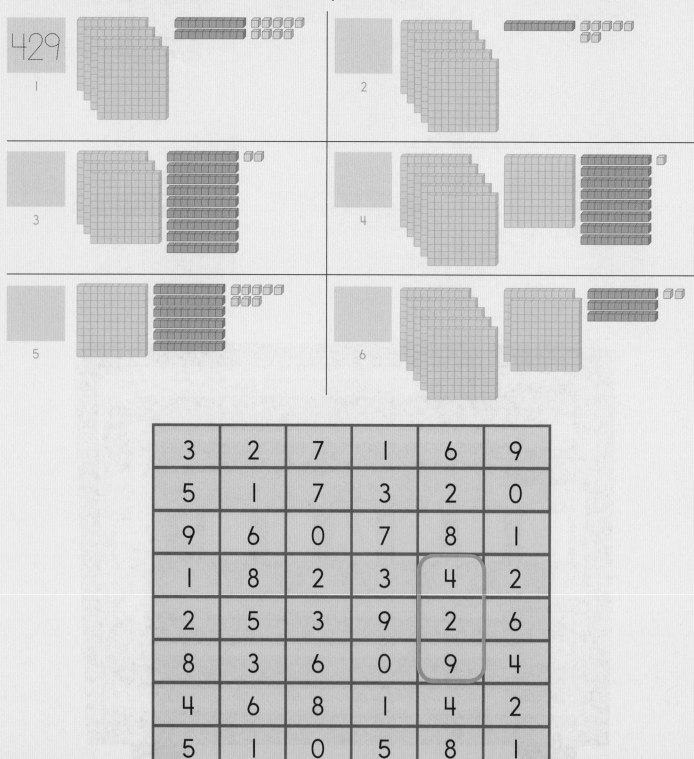

3	2	7	1	6	9
5	1	7	3	2	0
9	6	0	7	8	1
1	8	2	3	4	2
2	5	3	9	2	6
8	3	6	0	9	4
4	6	8	1	4	2
5	1	0	5	8	1

Code Breaker

WRITE the number for each picture. Then WRITE the letter that matches each number to solve the riddle.

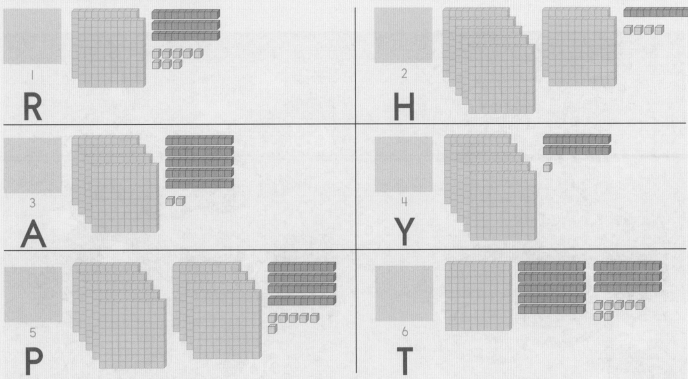

R

H

A

Y

P

T

What did the pirate wear to his birthday party?

452

946 452 238 238 238 187 521

714 452 187 .

Stepping Stones

START at the arrow. DRAW a path by counting up from 53 to reach the bunny.

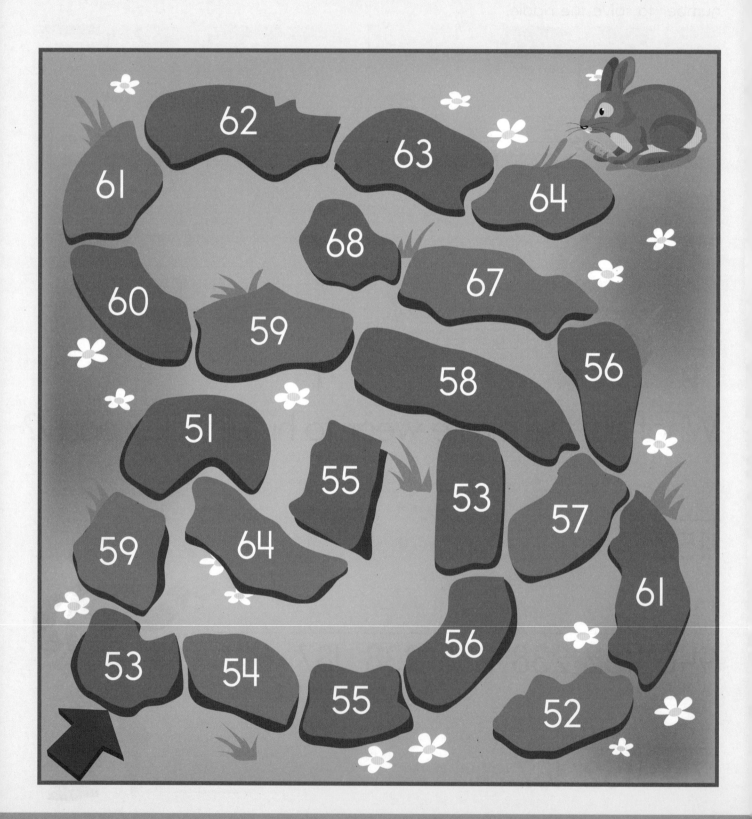

Where's My Brain?

START at the arrow. DRAW a path by skip counting by 2 to reach the brain.

HINT: Skip counting is like adding 2 to each number. For example: 1, 3, 5, 7, and so on.

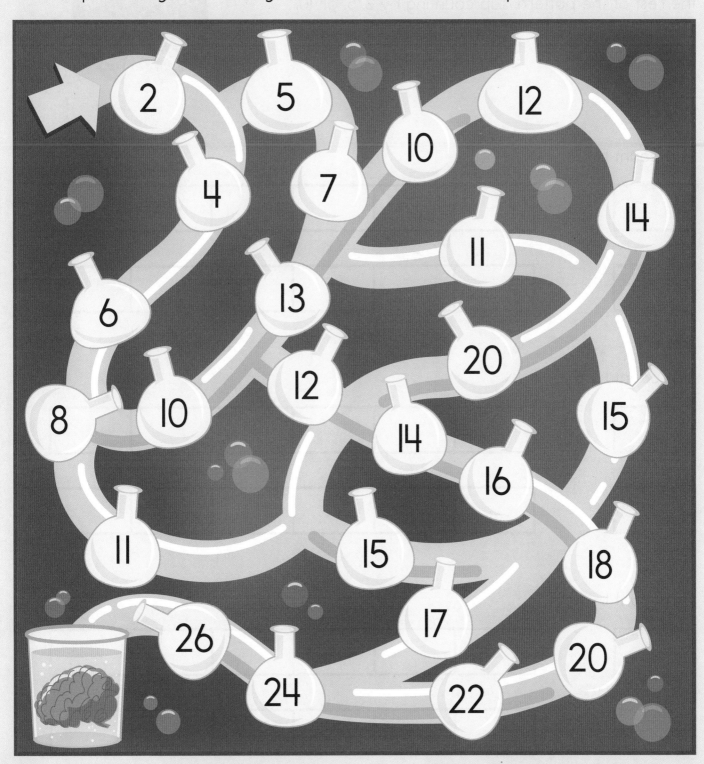

Spin It

Use the spinner from page 362. SPIN the spinner, and WRITE the number in the first box. Then WRITE the rest of the pattern, skip counting by 2, 5, or 10. (Save the spinner to use again.)

Skip count by 2:

Skip count by 5:

Skip count by 10:

Roll It

ROLL a number cube, and WRITE the
number in the first box. ROLL it again
and write the number in the second box.
Then WRITE the next six numbers, skip
counting by the difference between the
first two numbers.

Example:

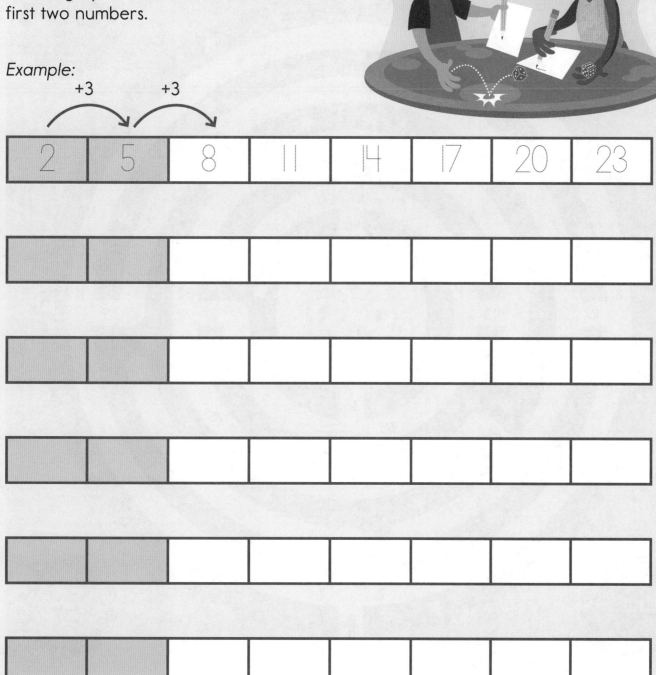

+3   +3

| 2 | 5 | 8 | 11 | 14 | 17 | 20 | 23 |

Find the Fountain

START at the arrow, and DRAW the correct path to the center fountain.
When there is a choice of numbers, follow the smaller number.

10

Just Right

WRITE each number next to a smaller blue number.

HINT: There may be more than one place to put a number, but you need to use every number.

28   71   55   83   ~~20~~   46   66   12   99   76

13   20
        1

58
        3

93
        5

46
        7

75
        9

67
        2

4
        4

22
        6

80
        8

31
        10

Find the Fountain

START at the arrow, and DRAW the correct path to the center fountain.
When there is a choice of numbers, follow the larger number.

Win Big

Wherever two boxes point to one box, WRITE the larger number. START at the sides and work toward the center to see which number will win big.

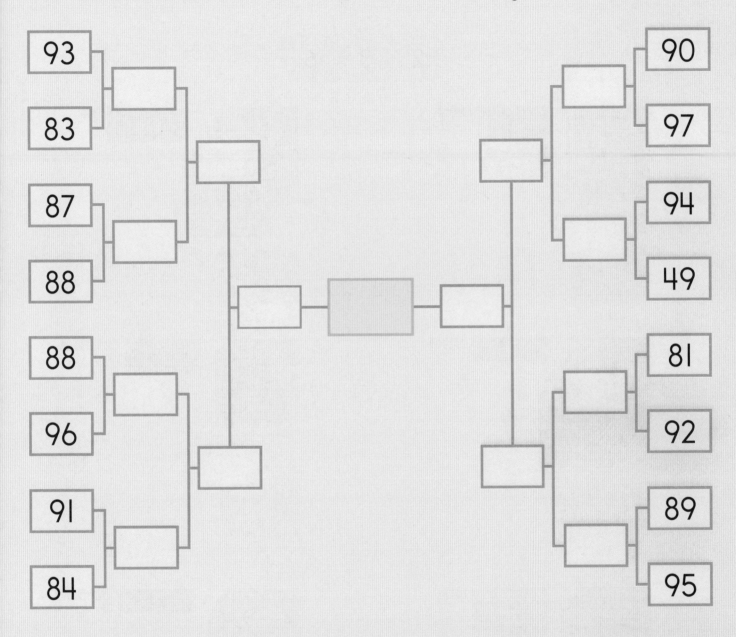

93

83

87

88

88

96

91

84

90

97

94

49

81

92

89

95

Cool Combinations

WRITE all of the different possible three-digit numbers you can make from the numbers 2, 3, and 6. Then CIRCLE the largest number.

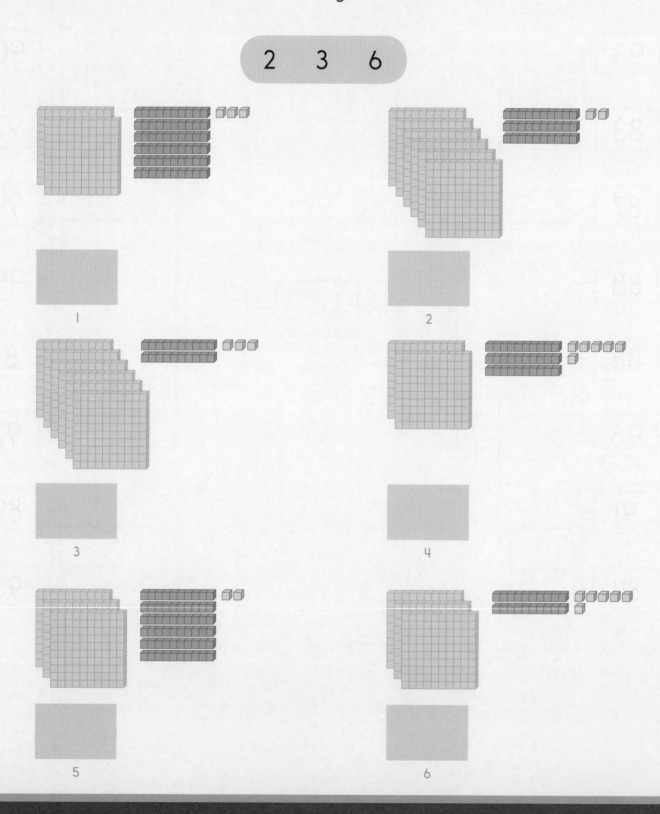

Skip to My Loo

SKIP COUNT by 2, 3, 4, and 5, and WRITE the numbers along each track.

Skip count by:

2	3	4	5
1	1	1	1
3			

Finish

Picture Perfect

DRAW different size rectangles to make buildings. Then DRAW doors and windows
and COLOR the buildings.

Hidden Shapes

FIND each shape hidden in the picture. DRAW a line to connect each shape with its location in the picture.

Doodle Pad

TRACE the shapes. Then DRAW a picture using each shape.

Trap the Circle

CONNECT the eight dots to draw one square inside the circle and one square outside the circle. Do not lift your pencil, and do not trace over any line already drawn.

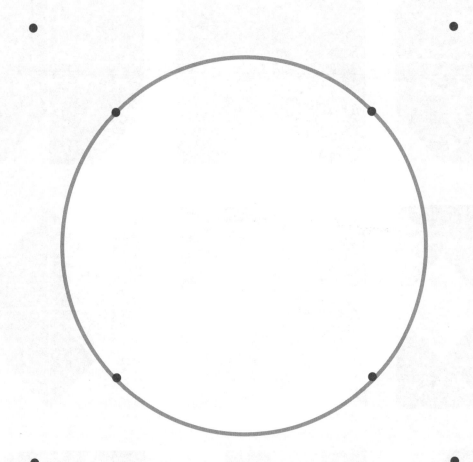

Turns and Transformations

CUT OUT the 12 cards on page 307, and ARRANGE them to make each shape shown on this page.

Sneaky Shapes

WRITE the number of triangles and rectangles you see.

HINT: Think about the different ways smaller shapes can make larger shapes, like when four small triangles make a larger triangle.

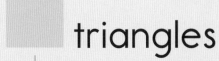 triangles

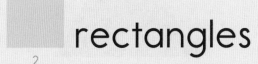 rectangles

Shape Shifters

A shape has **symmetry** if a line can divide the shape so each half is a mirror image of the other. Use the pattern block pieces from page 363, and PLACE the pieces to make each picture symmetrical without overlapping any pieces. (Save the pattern block pieces to use again.)

Invisible Illusions

COLOR the picture symmetrically. When you are done coloring, LOOK on the picture. Do you see the symmetry?

Incredible Illusions

COLOR the picture so it is symmetrical. When you're done coloring, LOOK at the picture. Do you see two faces or a candlestick?

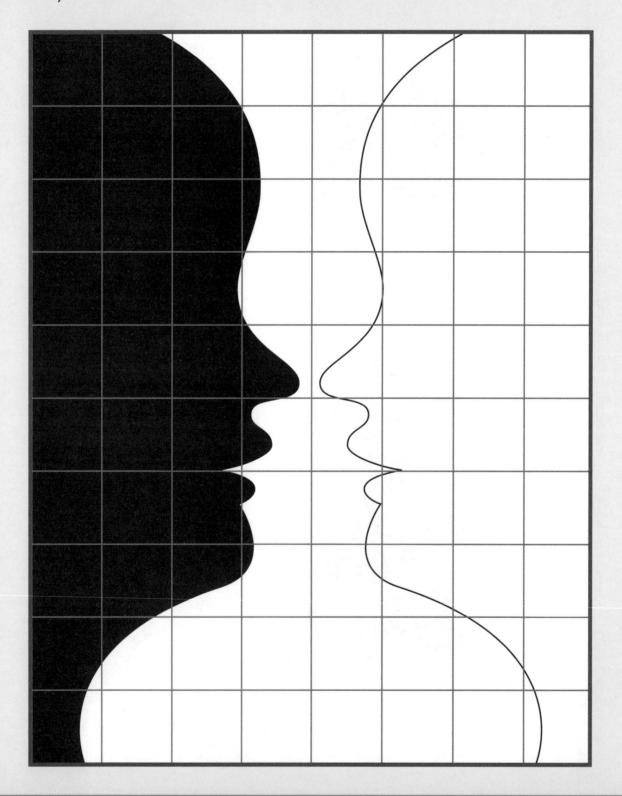

Cool Kaleidoscope

COLOR the kaleidoscope so it is symmetrical.

HINT: Work across the top, then make the bottom a mirror image of the top.

Tricky Tangrams

Use the tangram pieces from page 365, and PLACE the pieces to completely fill each shape. (Save the pieces to use again.)

HINT: Try placing the largest pieces first.

Shape Shifters

Use the pattern block pieces from page 363, and PLACE the pieces to completely fill each shape without overlapping any pieces. See if you can solve the puzzles different ways. (Save the pieces to use again.)

Odd Way Home

Michael lives in the house with a star on it, and he is playing a game on his ride home. He only wants to make right turns, and he doesn't want to ride past any red houses. DRAW a line to show his way home.

Shape Shifters

Use the pattern block pieces from page 363, and PLACE the pieces to make this shape four different ways without overlapping any pieces. Can you think of even more ways to make this shape?

PLACE the pieces to make the picture symmetrical without overlapping any pieces.

House Hunt

HUNT around your home to FIND eight things longer than this line of 5 paper clips. WRITE what you find.

House Hunt

HUNT around your home to FIND eight things shorter than this line of 10 ants.
WRITE what you find.

Caterpillar Coins

Each caterpillar is four coins long. MEASURE each caterpillar with a line of four quarters, dimes, nickels, and pennies. When you find a match, WRITE the name of the coin.

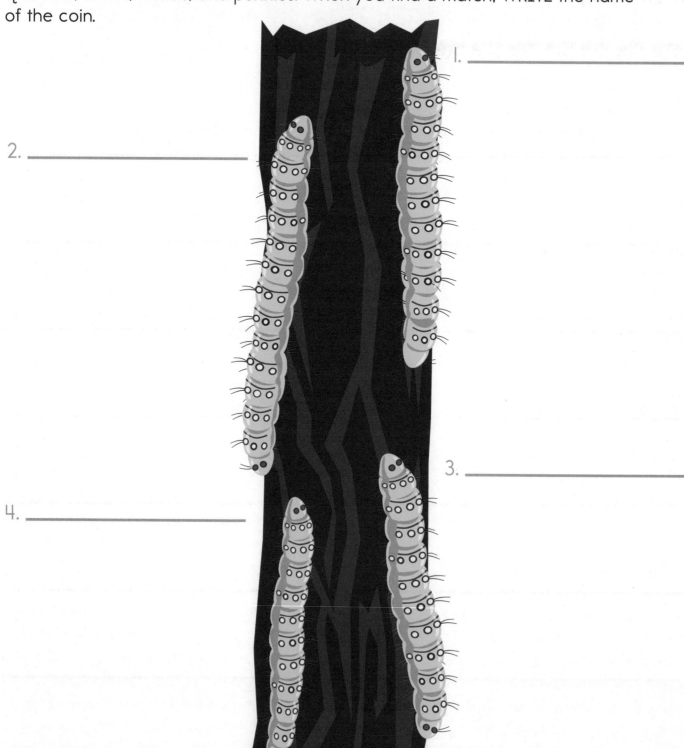

1. _____

2. _____

3. _____

4. _____

Toothy the Shark

MEASURE the length of each tooth in centimeters. DRAW lines connecting pairs of teeth that are the same length.

Coming Closest

WRITE the numbers 1 through 6 on the asteroids so that 1 is the asteroid you think is closest to the planet and 6 is the asteroid you think is farthest away. Then MEASURE in inches to see if you're correct.

Incredible Illusions

Does the blue line or the green line look longer? CIRCLE the line that looks longer in each pair. Then MEASURE each line in inches to compare.

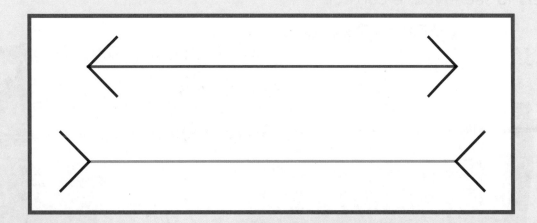

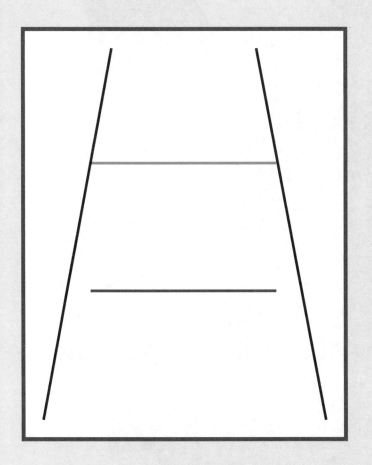

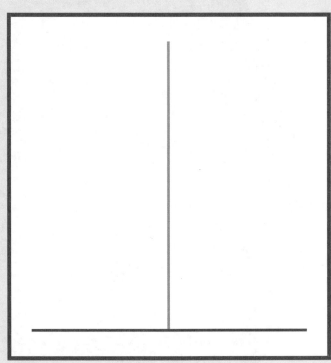

So Far Away

WRITE the numbers 1 through 8 next to the fireflies so that 1 is the firefly you think is closest to the light and 8 is the firefly you think is farthest away. Then MEASURE in centimeters to see if you're correct.

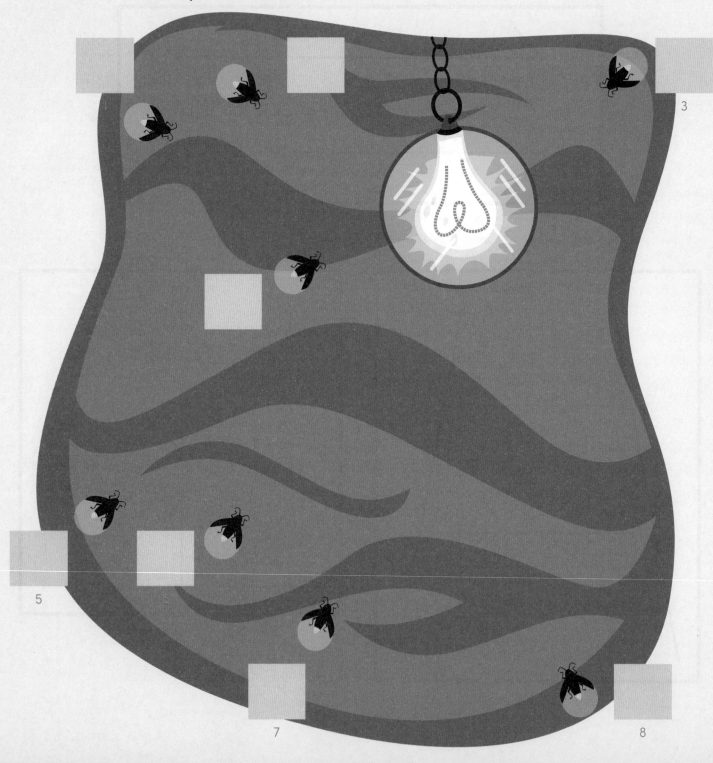

3

5

7

8

Don't Go Over

GUESS the distance between each pair of bugs in centimeters. Then MEASURE the distance. For every centimeter in the difference between the two measurements, COLOR a section on the chart. If you get through the whole page without filling the chart, you win!

HINT: To find the difference, subtract the smaller number from the larger number.

1.

Guess: _____ Check: _____

2.

Guess: _____ Check: _____

3.

Guess: _____ Check: _____

4.

Guess: _____ Check: _____

5.

Guess: _____ Check: _____

Telling Time in Hours

Mystery Time

COLOR the times in the picture according to the color of the clocks at the top.
When you are done coloring, WRITE the mystery time under the picture.

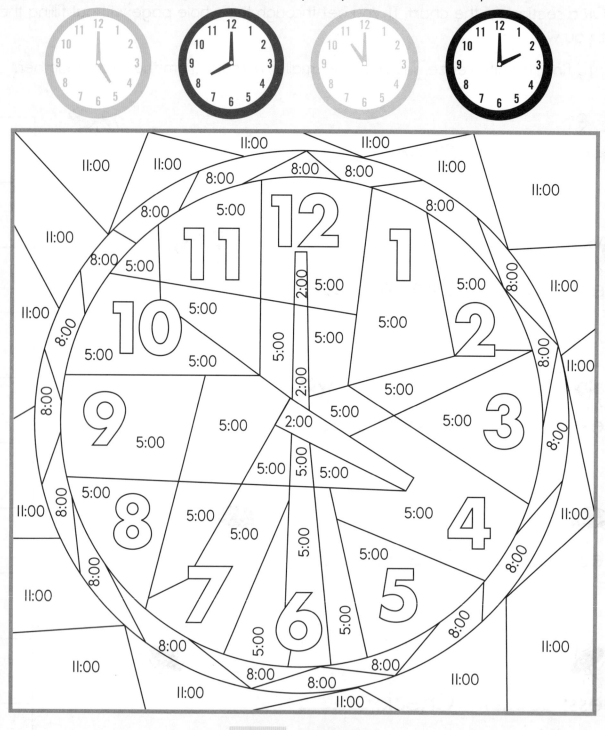

:00

Make a Match

CUT OUT the times and clocks. READ the rules. PLAY the game!
(Save these cards for use with page 342.)

Rules: Two players
1. Place the cards face down on a table.
2. Take turns turning over two cards at a time.
3. Keep the cards when you match a clock and a time.

The player with the most matches wins!

1:00		3:00	
4:00		6:00	
7:00		9:00	
10:00		12:00	

Around the Clock

Use the clock hands from page 365 and the spinner from page 362. SPIN the spinner, then PLACE the pieces to make that time on the clock.

HINT: Add "o'clock" to each number you spin on the spinner to name the time.

Mystery Time

COLOR the times in the picture according to the color of the clocks at the top. When you are done coloring, WRITE the mystery time under the picture.

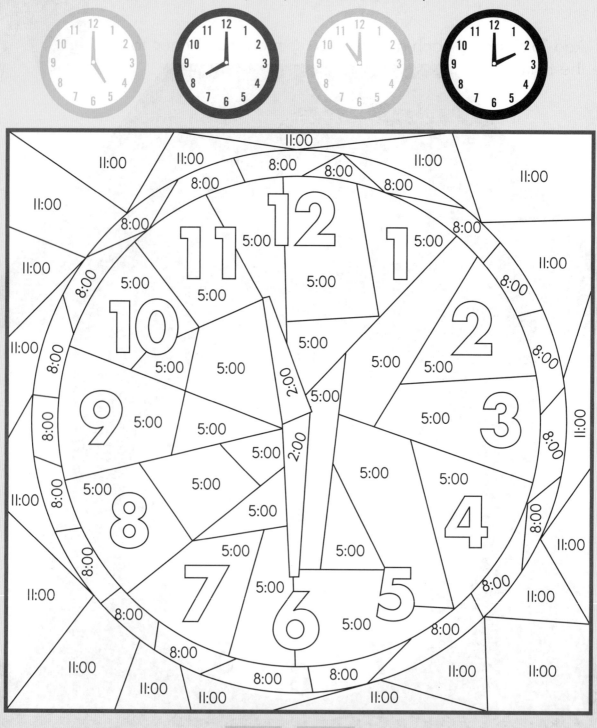

Make a Match

CUT OUT the times and clocks. READ the rules. PLAY the game!

HINT: Combine these with the cards from page 339 for a greater challenge.

Rules: Two players
1. Place the cards face down on a table.
2. Take turns turning over two cards at a time.
3. Keep the cards when you match a clock and a time.

The player with the most matches wins!

1:30		2:30	
3:30		5:30	
6:30		8:30	
11:30		12:30	

Time Travel

DRAW a line from Start through the clocks to get to the end, traveling ahead one hour as you go from clock to clock.

Start

End

What's My Time?

READ the clues, and CIRCLE the clock with the correct time.

I'm next to at least one clock that is later than I am.

I'm not usually a time when you would eat a meal.

If I'm at night, you're probably asleep.

I'm a half hour later than one of my neighbors.

Time Travel

DRAW a line from Start through the clocks to get to the end, traveling ahead two and a half hours as you go from clock to clock.

Start

End

Code Breaker

WRITE the value of each coin or coin set. Then WRITE the letter that matches each value to solve the riddle.

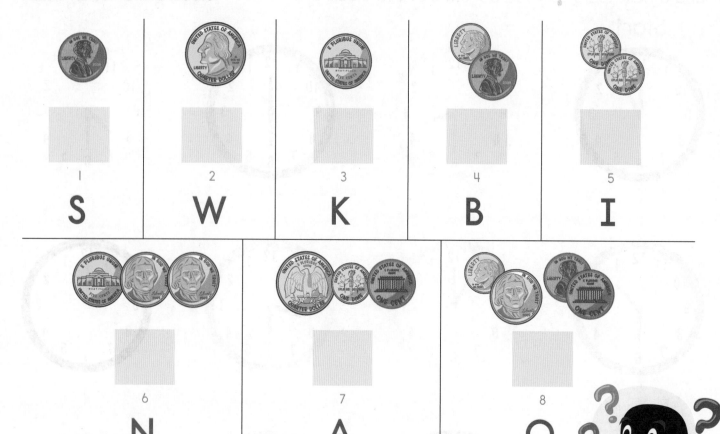

1	2	3	4	5
S	W	K	B	I

6	7	8
N	A	O

Where does the penguin keep his money?

___ ___ ___ ___ ___ ___ ___
20¢ 15¢   36¢   1¢ 15¢ 17¢ 25¢

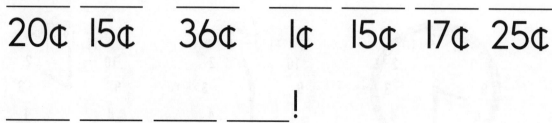

___ ___ ___ ___ !
11¢ 36¢ 15¢ 5¢

Make a Match

CUT OUT the pictures. READ the rules. PLAY the game!

Rules: Two players
1. Place the cards face down on a table.
2. Take turns turning over two cards at a time.
3. Keep the cards when you match coins with the same value.

The player with the most matches wins!

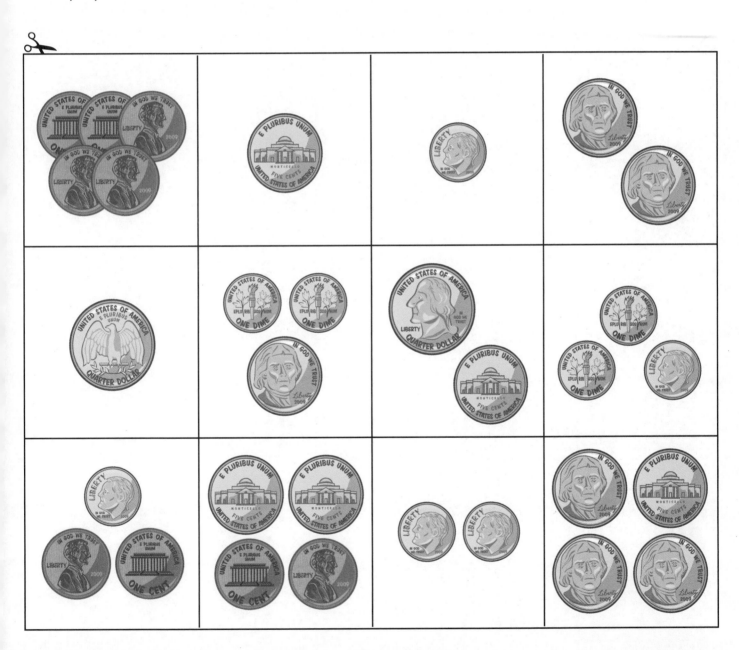

Coin Values

Pocket Change

DRAW exactly two lines to create four different sets of coins of equal value.

Slide Sort

CIRCLE the coins that are **not** enough money to pay for the object at the bottom of the slide.

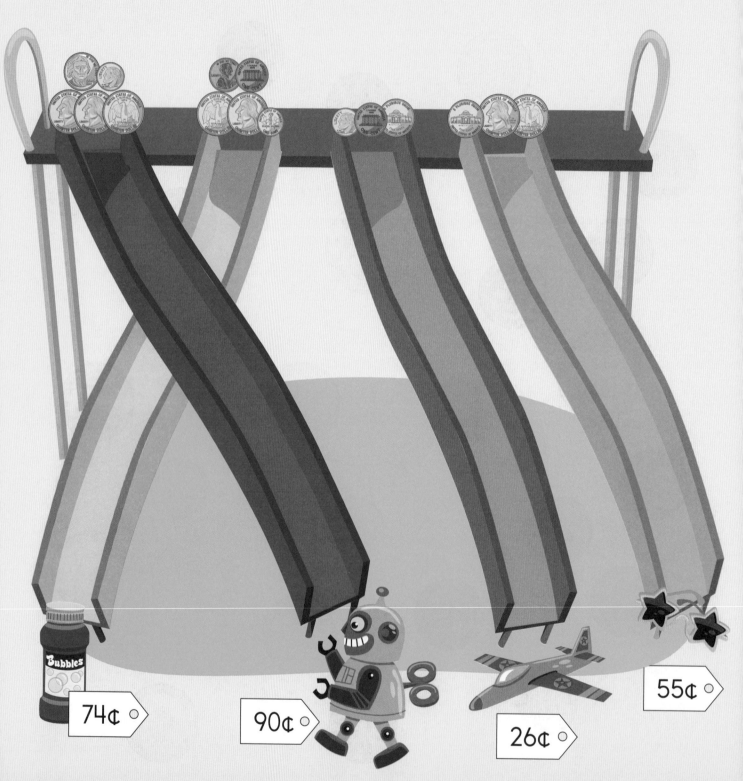

Make a Buck

CUT OUT the cards. READ the rules. PLAY the game!

Rules: Two players
1. Place the cards face down in a stack on a table.
2. Take turns picking a card.
3. Keep turning cards until your coins total one dollar or more.
   How many different ways can you make a dollar?

The first player to make a dollar wins!

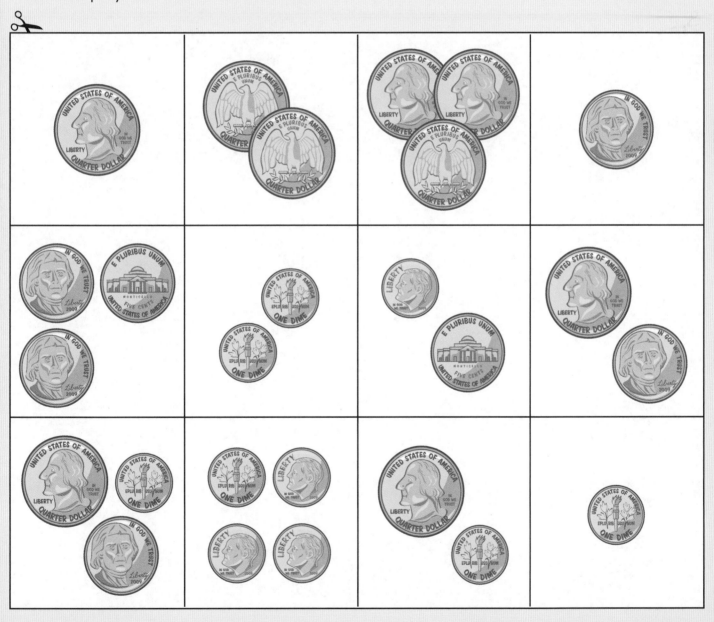

Money Maze

DRAW a line to get from the start of the maze to the end, crossing exactly enough coins to total the end amount.

HINT: There's more than one way through the maze, but you must follow the path that totals 82¢.

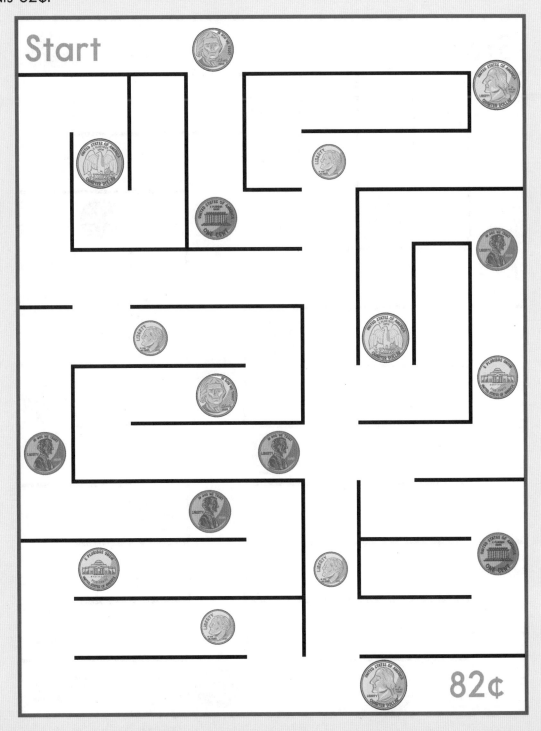

Start

82¢

Money Maze

DRAW a line to get from the start of the maze to the end, crossing exactly enough coins to total the end amount.

HINT: There's more than one way through the maze, but you must follow the path that totals 99¢.

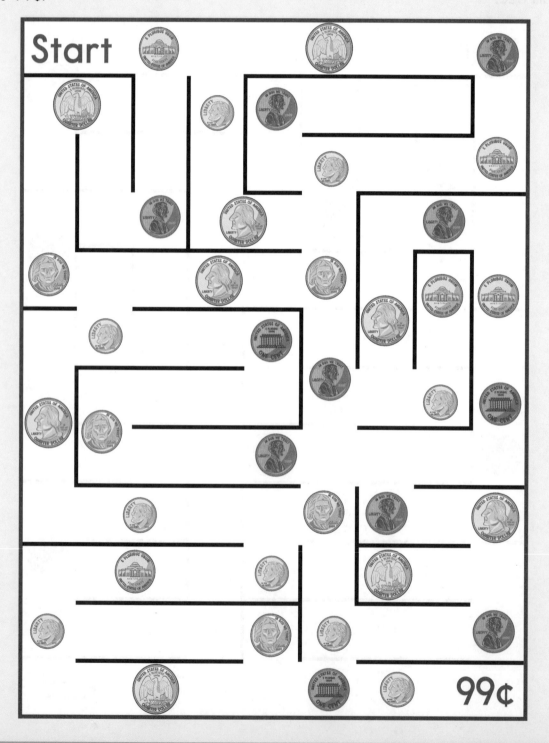

Dominoes

CUT OUT the dominoes.

These dominoes are for use with pages 252 and 274.

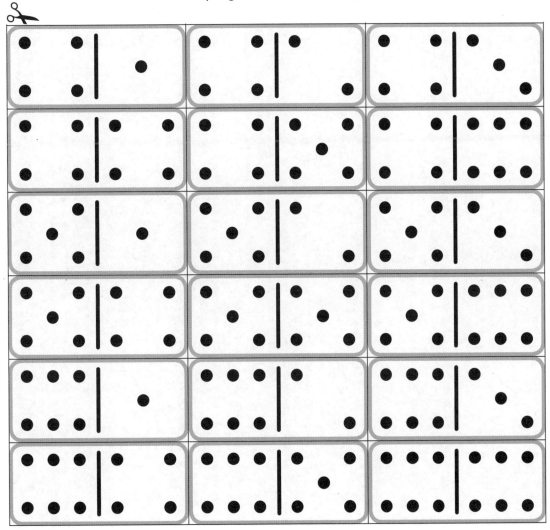

Pattern Blocks

CUT OUT the 31 pattern block pieces.

These pattern block pieces are for use with pages 310, 311, 316, 317, and 323.

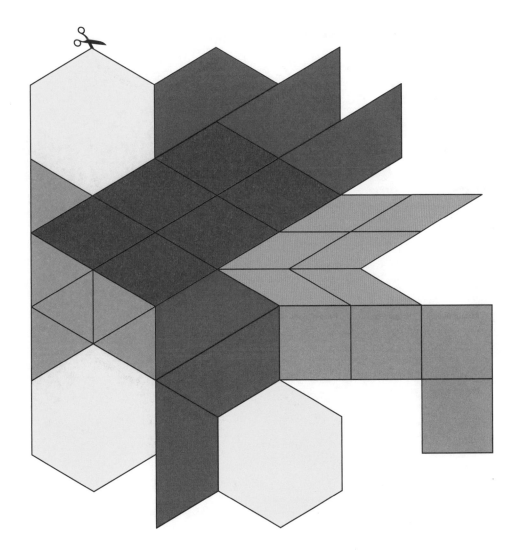

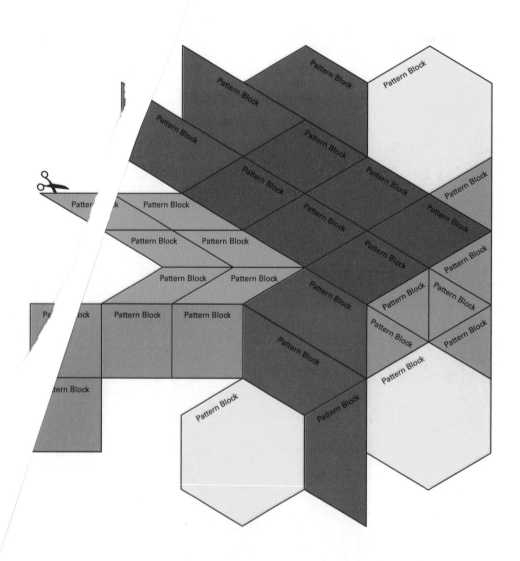

Page 250

Page 251

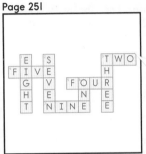

Page 252
Have someone check
your answers.

Page 253
1. 7   2. 6
3. 5   4. 2
5. 9   6. 8
Combination: 2 5 6 7 8 9

Page 254

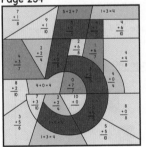

Page 255
Have someone check
your answers.

Page 256
Have someone check
your answers.

Page 257
1. 4   2. 10
3. 9   4. 6
5. 8   6. 1
7. 5   8. 7
9. 3
BECAUSE 7 8 9!

Page 258

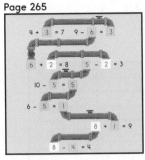

Page 259
1. 2   2. 4
3. 3   4. 8
5. 6   6. 0
Combination: 8 6 4 3 2 0

Page 260
Have someone check
your answers.

Page 261
1. 5   2. 1
3. 4   4. 2
5. 0

Page 262

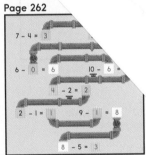

Page 263
8 + 1 = 9
1 + 8 = 9
9 – 8 = 1
9 – 1 = 8

5 + 4 = 9
4 + 5 = 9
9 – 5 = 4
9 – 4 = 5

6 + 3 = 9
3 + 6 = 9
9 – 6 = 3
9 – 3 = 6

Page 264

1	2	3	4		3	4	2	1
3	4	1	2		1	2	4	3
2	1	4	3		2	3	1	4
4	3	2	1		4	1	3	2

1	9	2	4	5	6	3	7	8
7	3	4	9	2	8	1	5	6
6	5	8	7	3	1	9	2	4
4	2	1	3	6	9	7	8	5
5	6	9	8	7	4	2	1	3
8	7	3	5	1	2	6	4	9
2	4	7	6	9	5	8	3	1
3	8	6	1	4	7	5	9	2
9	1	5	2	8	3	4	6	7

Page 265

Page 266

Page 267

T W
FIFTEEN
O
EEN

Page 269

15 Ants   16 Ants
18 Ants   14 Ants

Page 270
1. 15   2. 20
3. 12   4. 11
5. 18   6. 14
Combination: 11 12 14 15 18 20

Page 271
Have someone check
your answers.

Page 272
Have someone check
your answers.

Page 273
1. 13   2. 19
3. 11   4. 15
5. 18   6. 20
7. 14   8. 12
9. 16
AT THE MOOVIES!

Page 274
Have someone check
your answers.

Page 275

Page 276
1. 12   2. 6
3. 9   4. 18
5. 5   6. 1
Combination: 18 12 9 6 5 1

Page 277
Have someone check
your answers.

Page 278
             2. 11
             4. 9

Answers

Page 281

11 + 6 = 17
6 + 11 = 17
17 − 11 = 6
17 − 6 = 11

15 + 2 = 17
2 + 15 = 17
17 − 15 = 2
17 − 2 = 15

14 + 3 = 17
3 + 14 = 17
17 − 14 = 3
17 − 3 = 14

Page 282
Suggestion:

2	9	4
7	5	3
6	1	8

Page 283

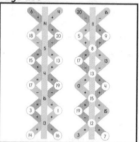

Pages 284–285

Pages 286–287
THE SECRET PLANS ARE HIDDEN IN THE VASE ON THE DESK.

Page 288

Page 289
1. 43   2. 18
3. 52   4. 61
5. 36   6. 29
Combination: 6 5 4 3 2 1

Page 290
1. 429   2. 517
3. 392   4. 681
5. 168   6. 732

3	2	7	1	6	9
5	1	7	3	2	0
9	6	0	7	8	1
1	8	2	3	4	2
2	5	3	9	2	6
8	3	6	0	9	4
4	6	8	1	4	2
5	1	0	5	8	1

Page 291
1. 238   2. 714
3. 452   4. 521
5. 946   6. 187
A PARRRTY HAT.

Page 292

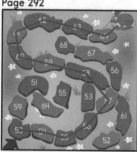

Page 293

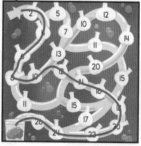

Page 294
Have someone check your answers.

Page 295
Have someone check your answers.

Page 296

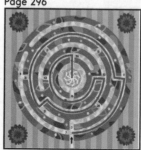

Page 297
1. 20   2. 71
3. 66   4. 12
5. 99   6. 28
7. 55   8. 83
9. 76   10. 46

Page 298

Page 299

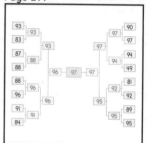

Page 300
1. 263   2. 632
3. 623   4. 236
5. 362   6. 326
Biggest number: 632

Page 301

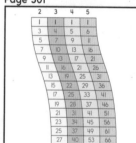

2	3	4	5
1	1	1	
3	4	5	6
5	7	9	11
7	10	13	16
9	13	17	21
11	16	21	26
13	19	25	31
15	22	29	36
17	25	33	41
19	28	37	46
21	31	41	51
23	34	45	56
25	37	49	61
27	40	53	66

Page 302
Have someone check your answers.

Page 303

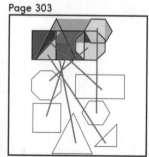

Page 304
Have someone check your answers.

Page 305
Suggestion:
First connect the four dots on the circle to make a square.

Then connect the last dot of the square to a dot on the outside of the circle.

Finally, draw the second square around the circle.

Page 306
Have someone check your answers.

Page 309
1. 13   2. 9

Page 310

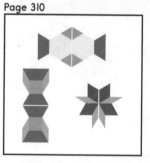

Page 311

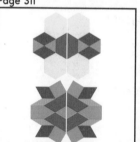

Page 312

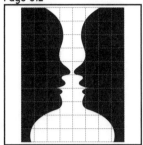

Page 313

Page 314
Suggestion:

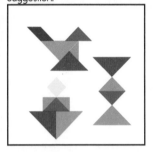

Page 315
Suggestion:

Page 316
Suggestion:

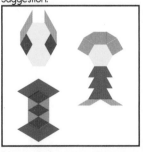

Page 317
Suggestion:

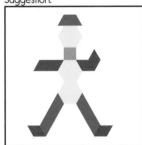

Page 318

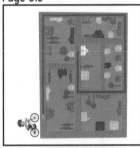

Page 319

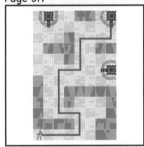

Pages 320–321
1. B7   2. E7
3. D5   4. A5
5. C3   6. DI
7. A2   8. E3
9. BI

Page 322
Suggestion:

Page 323
Suggestion:

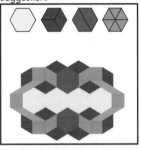

Page 324
Have someone check
your answers.

Page 325
Have someone check
your answers.

Page 326
1. nickel
2. quarter
3. penny
4. dime

Page 327

Page 328
An INCHWORM.

Page 329

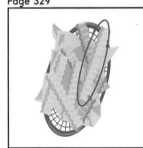

Page 330
SO LONG!

Page 331

Page 332
1. I   2. 3
3. 2   4. 5
5. 4   6. 6

Page 333
Each pair of lines is the same length.

Page 334
1. 4   2. 3
3. 2   4. I
5. 7   6. 5
7. 6   8. 8

Page 335
Check:
1. 4   2. 5
3. 10   4. 7
5. 6   6. 9

Page 336

Page 337
Check:
1. 12   2. 9
3. 6   4. 8
5. 10

Page 338

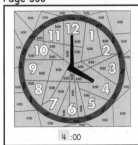

Answers

Page 339
Have someone check
your answers.

Page 341
Have someone check
your answers.

Page 342

11:30

Page 343
Have someone check
your answers.

Page 345

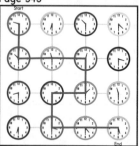

Page 346

Page 347

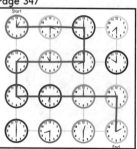

Page 348
I. Iȼ	2. 25ȼ
3. 5ȼ	4. IIȼ
5. 20ȼ	6. I5ȼ
7. 36ȼ	8. I7ȼ

IN A SNOW BANK!

Page 349
Have someone check
your answers.

Page 351

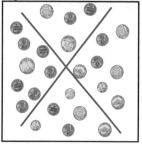

Page 352

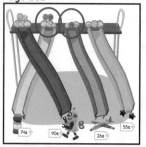

74ȼ   90ȼ   26ȼ   55ȼ

Page 353
Have someone check
your answers.

Page 355

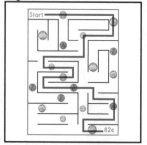

82ȼ

Page 356

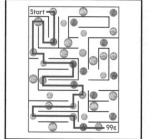

99ȼ